# The Great Court
## and The British Museum

# The Great Court

## and The British Museum

Robert Anderson

THE BRITISH MUSEUM PRESS

This book is dedicated to all who have played a part in the realization of the Great Court

The Trustees of The British Museum gratefully acknowledge generous assistance towards the production of this book from Dasha Shenkman

First published in 2000 by The British Museum Press
A division of The British Museum Company Ltd
46 Bloomsbury Street, London WC1B 3QQ

Third impression 2001

A catalogue record for this book is available from the British Library

ISBN 0 7141 2741 8

Designed by Isambard Thomas
Printed in England by Balding and Mansell

Construction of the Great
Court roof, early 2000

# Preface

THE GREAT COURT, dedicated to Her Majesty Queen Elizabeth II and opened at the end of 2000, has been the largest building project taken on by the British Museum since the completion of Sir Robert Smirke's edifice in Greek Revival style in 1850. It is one of a large number of ambitious museum and gallery schemes undertaken in London and elsewhere around the turn of the millennium, arguably the most invigorating period of museum development since the late nineteenth century. In a pioneering work of 1965 by Michael Brawne, *Neue Museen*, forty-one new developments were listed. Of these, only two were British: the Commonwealth Institute in London and Christ Church Picture Gallery in Oxford. If the book were to be written today, the proportion of British museums qualifying for inclusion on architectural grounds would certainly be greater. It is now generally considered that museums can be a popular and powerful cultural resource which can be exploited further by making appropriate investments in their future, new buildings included.

The British Museum started to make detailed preparations for its Great Court building programme in 1993. An early decision taken was that the Museum must stay open throughout the site operations, even though on occasion the Museum and its visitors would have to endure the most trying conditions. It is a tribute to the tolerance of the public, and to the efforts of staff and building contractors alike, that nearly all Museum activities continued without too much disruption being felt. The Museum believes that a high level of service was maintained, despite the difficult months and years. Now that the project is complete, many deserve thanks for their contributions: donors, benefactors, supporters, statutory bodies, central and local government officials, lottery bodies, Trustees and staff. Additionally, there are those involved directly in the day-to-day work: architects, surveyors, contractors and builders, without whose skill and dedication the Great Court could not have been built. Likewise, this book could not have been produced without skilful help. I would like to thank those who have provided valuable material, namely Fran Dunkels, Gerard Ford and Peter Buchanan. Gratitude is due to Marjorie Caygill and Julia Walton of the Director's Office for their comments on the text and help with illustrations, many of which are photographs expertly taken by the British Museum Photographic Service, and to Coralie Hepburn of British Museum Press for producing this book so expeditiously.

*right*
View of the Great Court from the Centre Point building

*below*
HM The Queen, while visiting the Great Court on 31 March 1999, with (left) Dr Robert Anderson, Director of the British Museum; (right) Chris Jones, client sponsor; and (partly hidden) Graham Greene, Chairman of Trustees

*bottom*
HM The Queen at the opening of the Great Court on 6 December 2000, with (from left) Graham Greene, Lord Foster, Dr Robert Anderson (above) and Spencer de Grey (right)

# Inception

Alfred Stevens' unrealized
decorative scheme for the
Reading Room,
*Illustrated London News*, 1857

Lord Foster (left) and Dr Robert Anderson on the 'snow gallery' of the Reading Room dome, July 1994

S UCCESSFUL MUSEUMS are never static institutions. They not only innovate but they also constantly have to evolve to take heed of the changing demands, in terms of both size and type, that are placed on them. Original buildings soon become inadequate for fast-developing requirements. As museums incessantly accumulate collections (and nearly all do, that is their job), they require increasing amounts of space for storage and for conservation. The building up of collections leads to ambitions for increased display facilities. Approaches to display change. More background information is provided and objects are no longer expected to 'speak for themselves' to all visitors. The rise of the special exhibition phenomenon, from the more modest to the 'blockbuster', results in an adjustment of emphasis from the permanent towards the temporary. The uses to which museums are put has changed with time. The demand from schools and colleges for educational facilities has meant that specialized areas are needed for teaching, for undertaking projects, for coats and bags, and for refreshment. The scope of museum education for adults has expanded beyond its earlier, narrow aspiration to embrace the concept of lifelong learning, for which further space is needed. Museums often host academic conferences, which require seminar rooms for scholarly debate and spaces for receptions (to allow for the cross-fertilization of ideas). The nature of the museum visit has changed. Visitors now expect to have restaurants and cafés available, and they frequently want to purchase books about and reproductions of the objects with which they have just come into contact. The museum shop has emerged as a distinct species, with a well-defined stock of merchandise. Museums are always short of money and to help raise income they are often hired out as fashionable venues for dinners, and for these, specialized facilities are needed. The demographic background of visitors to national museums has changed: the majority are no longer local, but fly in from around the world. As well as catering for tourists, museums have to take into account the particular needs of neighbouring ethnic communities, and those for whom museum-going has never been a habit. Museum guides and exhibition labels may well be found in languages other than English. In around 1990 the British Museum realized that it could only begin to meet these changing

public demands and fulfil its ambitions if substantial building developments were put in hand.

The end of the second millennium saw a remarkable increase in museum building, both in the creation of new museums and in the development of existing ones. In his 1976 study, *A History of Building Types*, Nikolaus Pevsner categorized buildings according to their function: government buildings, railway stations, hospitals and so on. In each chapter he traced the history of a particular type of building, one of which was the museum, and it is telling how little he had to say about museum development after the 1930s. This situation was to change, however, in the 1990s, a decade that saw the flourishing of museums as a building type, with architects of the calibre of I.M. Pei, James Stirling and Richard Meier being commissioned to construct and adapt a variety of museums around the world. One only has to think of the Louvre pyramid, the Staatsgalerie in Stuttgart and the Getty Centre in Los Angeles to name but three masterful examples of their work.

In Great Britain the financial support needed for museum ambitions from the mid-1990s was on many occasions provided by funds derived from the National Lottery, in particular those available from the Millennium Commission and the Heritage Lottery Fund. This is true for the Great Court of the British Museum, which arose as a result of wishing to satisfy the increasing and varied demands placed on the institution, and to provide visitors of all categories with a more enjoyable and rewarding experience. The highest possible standard of design was demanded by the Museum's Trustees and staff and they readily identified the proposals of Foster & Partners as the means of realizing their vision of a memorable modern building that would blend with the splendour of Sir Robert Smirke's neo-Grecian temple of antiquities. Everyone involved realized that the enterprise was dependant on the successful outcome of bids for lottery funds and on the generosity of private benefactors.

The British Museum has always occupied the same site, ever since it was established following the death of the physician and collector *extraordinaire*, Sir Hans Sloane. Money derived from a lottery held specifically for the purpose of setting up the Museum in 1753 was used to purchase a large mansion, Montagu House, in Bloomsbury, then on the northernmost edge of London. The house had originally been designed and built in 1675 by the Operator to the Royal Society, the ingenious Robert Hooke. However, it had burnt down eleven years later and was substantially rebuilt by a Frenchman, Puget, about whom nothing else is known. The British Museum, in Montagu House, opened its doors to the public in January 1759, having been filled with Sloane's eclectic collection, together with a number of other collections of books and manuscripts for which the government required a home. It is no surprise that by the early years of the nineteenth century the space had become inadequate, the rapidly developing collections of classical antiquities and natural history placing a particular strain on the system.

By 1802 the growing lack of space could no longer be ignored and the Museum planned an expansion northwards into the gardens of Montagu House. In the event, George Saunders' Townley Gallery of 1808, designed to house the newly acquired Egyptian sculptures and the Graeco-Roman collections of Charles Townley, was the only part of the scheme to be realized. This in itself did not solve the continuing space problem, and in 1816 the renowned architect Sir Robert Smirke was called in at the very time when the Museum acquired the Parthenon sculptures brought from Greece by Lord Elgin. In 1821 Smirke recommended that two parallel wings should be built to the north, but then, in 1823, the problem grew even more severe when King George IV decided to transfer the library of his father, King George III, to the Museum. It was at this time that the concept of the building that was finally constructed first emerged. Smirke proposed to build a quadrangle, one of whose sides would comprise Montagu House. When this had been completed, Montagu house itself would be demolished, and a new southern building, with elaborate portico, would be constructed to complete the Museum. Enclosed by the quadrangle would be a large courtyard, two acres in extent. This would be used as an open space, a garden in fact, where the public could wander during their visit. The concept was fully developed by the mid-1820s, even though the building was going to take a quarter century to complete. It was in the fashionable Greek Revival style, and yet it was innovative as a museum design. The portico's vast Ionic columns seem to have been inspired by

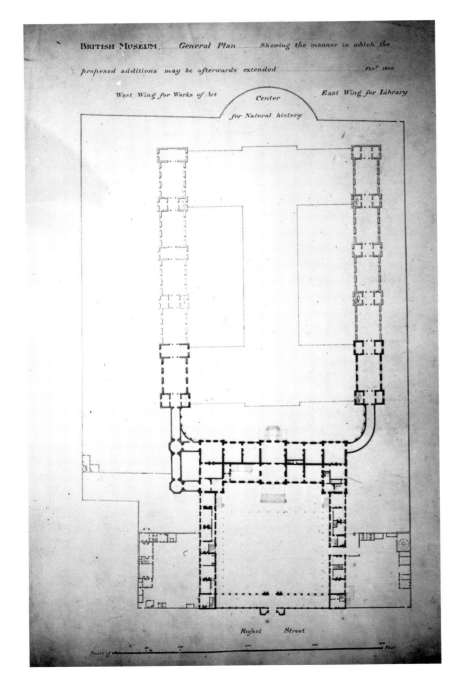

BRITISH MUSEUM.........General Plan.........Shewing the manner in which the

proposed additions may be afterwards extended.......................Feb.y 1805

West Wing for Works of Art

Center

for Natural history

East Wing for Library

Rufsel Street

Scale of

*left*
Proposal for extending Montagu House, plan by George Saunders, c. 1803

*right*
Robert Smirke's completed quadrangle, January 1852

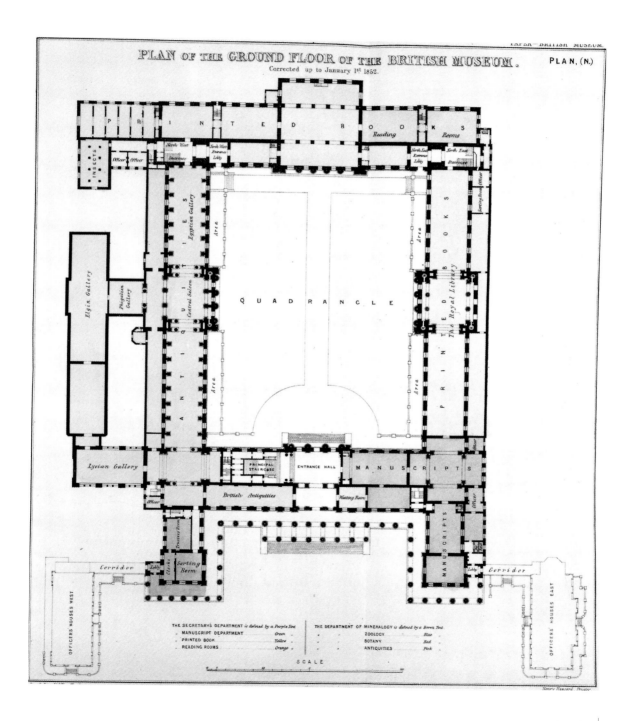

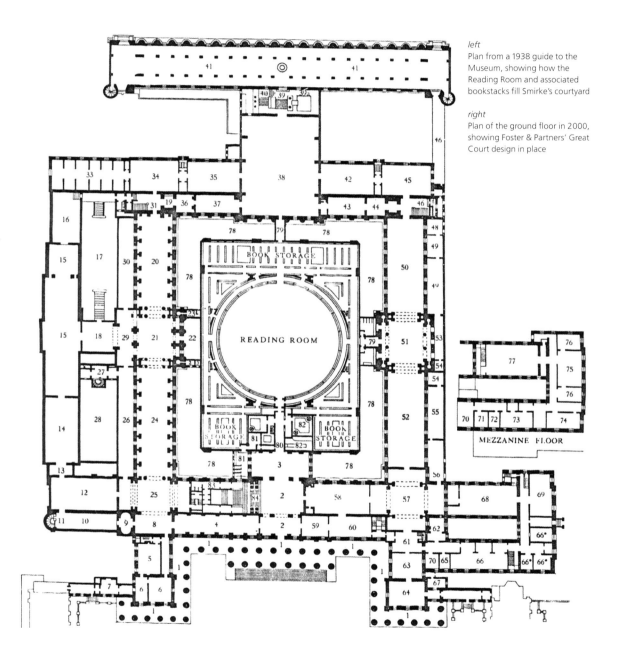

*left*
Plan from a 1938 guide to the
Museum, showing how the
Reading Room and associated
bookstacks fill Smirke's courtyard

*right*
Plan of the ground floor in 2000,
showing Foster & Partners' Great
Court design in place

READING ROOM

BOOK STORAGE

BOOK STORAGE

BOOK STORAGE

MEZZANINE FLOOR

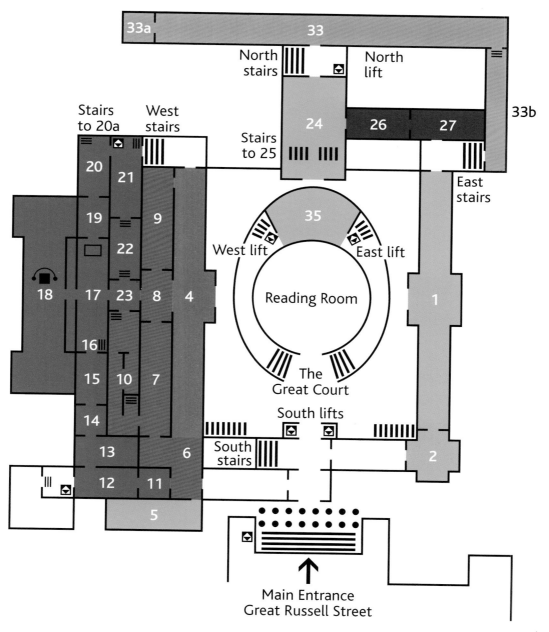

Montague Place Entrance

34

North stairs　North lift

33a　　　33　　　33b

North stairs　　North lift

Stairs to 20a　West stairs

Stairs to 25　24　26　27

East stairs

20　21

19　9

22

18　17　23　8　4　35

West lift　East lift

Reading Room

1

16

15　10　7

14

The Great Court

13　6　South lifts

South stairs

12　11　2

5

Main Entrance
Great Russell Street

those at the temple of Athena Polias at Priene in Asia Minor,
which Smirke may have known of from illustrations in the volume
*Antiquities of Ionia* published in 1769 by the Society of Dilettanti.

The first part of the grandiose scheme to be completed was the
King's Library, which was essentially a magnificent repository for
the books of King George III. This occupied the entire east side of
the quadrangle. Over the thirty years it took to complete Smirke's
building, and at the same time to demolish the ever-dwindling
remains of Montagu House, the Museum's collections expanded
enormously, with particularly large quantities of Egyptian, Greek,
Lycian and Assyrian excavated material arriving in Bloomsbury. To
accommodate this expansion, Smirke added further galleries
alongside the west range of the quadrangle. Hardly had the south
and final series of galleries, with adjacent portico, been
completed in 1848, than overspill accommodation in the form of
temporary sheds had to be erected on the colonnade. Pressure
mounted for the development of the central courtyard and
unsolicited suggestions were proposed, including one by William
Hosking, professor of architecture at King's College, London, who
put forward the idea of erecting within it a 'Rotunda for the
display of the finer and important works of sculpture'. Another
suggestion came in 1852 from Charles Barry, who had recently
completed his work on the new Houses of Parliament. He
proposed roofing over the courtyard with a glass canopy
supported on fifty pillars, to create a 'Hall of Antiquities'. Barry
submitted his proposal to the Museum's Trustees, in competition
with a scheme developed within the Museum by the Principal
Librarian, or Director, Antonio Panizzi. As Panizzi later wrote,
'schemes for covering over, or building in the quadrangle were
numberless'.

In a sense, the space crisis was in part created by Panizzi's
responsible attitude to book acquisition for the British Museum
Library. He had been appointed Keeper of Printed Books in 1837,
and established a determined programme of expansion for the
Library, both by strictly enforcing the Copyright Acts (which
required copies of all books to be deposited in the Museum by
their publishers) and by purchasing new material. During his first
ten years in office, the book stock nearly doubled in size. The
number of readers, and their demands, also increased

significantly. Thus Panizzi's building scheme was developed not
for the housing of antiquities but for the accommodation of
readers and for the storage of books. Panizzi's rough preliminary
sketches for a reading room in a circular building were worked up
into a formal architectural scheme by Sydney Smirke, who by
1846 had taken over from his brother as the principal architect of
the Museum. The innovative design comprised a drum
surmounted by a dome; within the room itself thirty-five reading
desks radiated from the centre like the spokes of a giant wheel.
The proposal was adopted by the Trustees in May 1852 and was
supported by a grant voted by Parliament in July 1854. Work
commenced on this building, which was placed nearly centrally in
the courtyard, that same year and by May 1857 it was ready to
receive its first readers. As part of the scheme, the space between
the outer drum of Sydney Smirke's Reading Room and the walls of
Robert Smirke's quadrangle was almost filled with four quadrant
bookstacks, each providing three floors of additional storage.
With the creation of one of the most renowned interiors in the

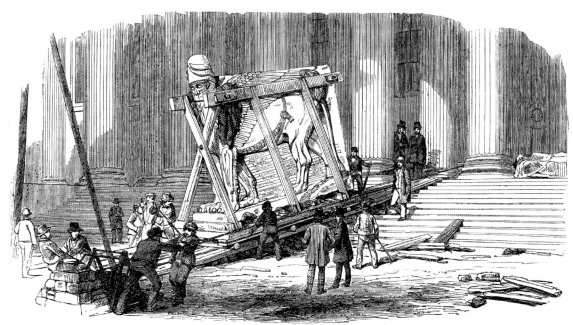

RECEPTION OF NINEVEH SCULPTURES AT THE BRITISH MUSEUM.

*above*
Facade overlooking Robert Smirke's quadrangle prior to the construction of the Reading Room, c. 1850

*above left*
Preparing to move the head of Ramesses II from the Townley Gallery to the new Egyptian Sculpture Gallery, June 1834

*left*
The arrival of a human-headed lion sculpture from Nimrud, *Illustrated London News*, 1852

*overleaf*
Constructing the Reading Room, photograph by William Lake Price, 1855

world (the exterior was only ever seen by a few Museum staff), the central courtyard, originally intended as a garden for visitors, was lost and forgotten.

Both the Smirke and Barry schemes embraced the use of cast iron as a building material. Its particular properties, including its ability to span long distances, the possibilities of prefabrication and the speed with which it could be erected, had all been exploited in Joseph Paxton's Great Exhibition building of 1851. In the Reading Room and its bookstacks 2,000 tons of cast iron were used. The dome had a diameter of 140 feet (42.6 metres), only 2 feet (61 cm) less than the dome of the Pantheon in Rome; it was supported entirely on twenty iron ribs spaced equidistantly around its circumference. The ribs themselves rose from a concrete foundation to the octangular lantern at the building's crown, restrained at intervals by cast-iron hoops that held the dome in shape. For its time, the Reading Room was of daring design. Although use of cast iron had been pioneered in a few earlier civil engineering projects, it was a relatively untried

material. In 1847 the cast-iron bridge over the River Dee in Scotland had collapsed, killing five people. After the accident, the government set up a Royal Commission on the Application of Iron to Railway Structures, the first public enquiry of its kind in the world. Many of the great engineers of the age were consulted, and opinions differed widely. Isambard Kingdom Brunel, who gave evidence, considered cast iron to be an 'uncertain material' when subject to tension. Yet Sydney Smirke remarked, 'Cast iron perfectly satisfies me of its excellence as a building material.' Even so, for the Reading Room cast iron was not perfect in all respects. Its properties were such that it put other materials from which the dome was constructed under great strain. The interior of the dome was constructed from a half-inch (1.27 cm) thick form of papier mâché called fibrous slab or patent wood, an invention patented in 1851 by Charles Bielefeld. It was made from pulped paper mixed with chalk and a setting plaster, and once pressed and rolled, it took on many of the characteristics of present-day fibre-based building board. Within the dome, panels of this material were attached to a wooden underframe, which was in turn fixed to the cast-iron skeleton. Surviving records show that from very early on, shrinkage of the fibrous slab, combined with the continual expansion and contraction of the cast-iron frame, which pulled and pushed the timber joists, resulted in a network of cracks appearing across the dome.

With the Reading Room and bookstacks in place, Robert Smirke's concept of the new Museum was lost. The ground floor of the north range of the quadrangle, being used by the Library, was never accessible to the general public, and to make a circuit of the Museum, stairs had to be climbed and descended in the north-west and north-east corners of the building. This problem was exacerbated when the King Edward VII Galleries and the associated Montague Place entrance were created early in the twentieth century: to move from north to south (or vice versa) inevitably involved an ascent and descent. Hidden from public view, the courtyard suffered many unsympathetic alterations and additions. In 1876 the inner portico of its south facade was demolished to extend the front entrance hall, while in 1936 windows in the north facade were enlarged to provide light for new mezzanine floors, a scheme developed by John Markham,

Cast-iron ribs and window frames of the Reading Room, 1855

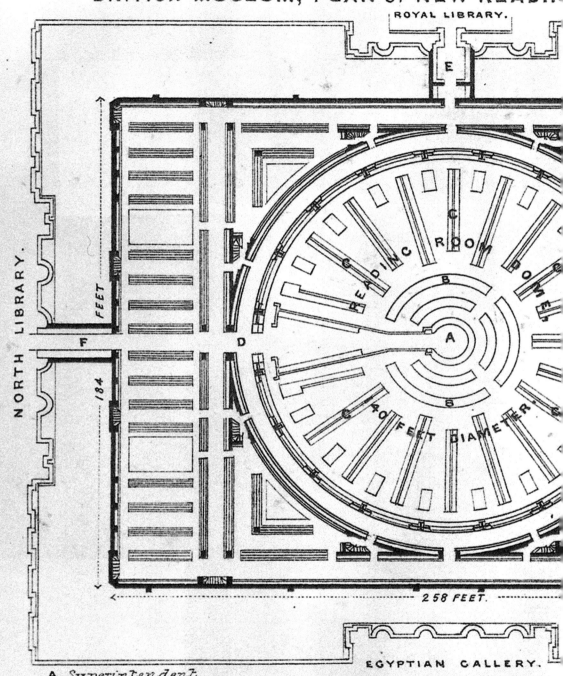

BRITISH MUSEUM, PLAN OF NEW READING

ROYAL LIBRARY.

E

NORTH LIBRARY.

FEET

184

F

D

READING ROOM DOME.

C

B

A

B

C

40 FEET DIAMETER.

258 FEET.

EGYPTIAN GALLERY.

A Superintendent.
B Catalogue Tables.
C Reader's Tables.
D Access for Attendants.
E Entrance from Royal Library

REFERENCE.

F Entrance from North Lib
G For Registration of Copyri
H Ladies Cloak Room.

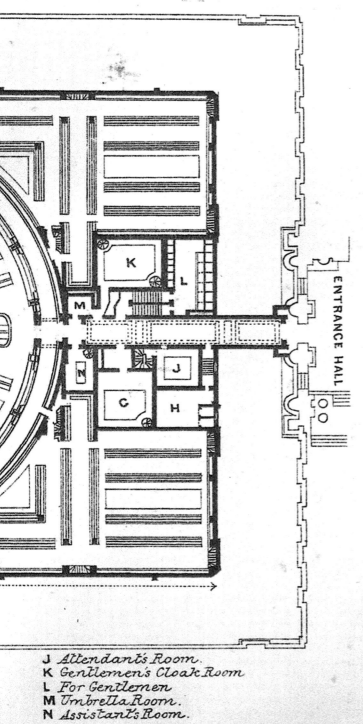

ENTRANCE HALL

J Attendant's Room.
K Gentlemen's Cloak Room
L For Gentlemen
M Umbrella Room.
N Assistant's Room.

Plan of the Reading Room and the
bookstacks that fill the courtyard
space, from an invitation to a
private view, 5 May 1857

Chief Architect to the Office of Works, that destroyed the integrity of Smirke's quadrangular concept. In 1920, to cope with the ever-increasing lack of storage space, a fourth storey was added to the south-east bookstack, an addition that was to put excessive strain on the iron structure. The other three stacks were left untouched until the 1930s, when those at the north-west and the north-east were rebuilt in response to a Royal Commission report on the problems faced by national museums that highlighted the lack of space. The stack in the south-west quadrant survived in its original state until hit by an incendiary bomb in 1941. It was then rebuilt in the 1950s.

To understand the evolution of the British Museum in terms of its buildings, another dimension has to be considered: the hiving-off of certain parts of the Museum to newly created institutions when strains on space simply became too great for adaptations or minor rebuilding to be effective. Although the British Museum played a small role in setting up the National Gallery in 1824 and the National Portrait Gallery in 1856, the move of the natural history collections to South Kensington in the 1880s had the most significant effect on the internal organization of the Museum galleries in the nineteenth century. In the twentieth century the event that would ultimately lead to Smirke's courtyard being redeveloped was the passing of the British Library Act in 1972. This separated off the Library departments of the British Museum to create a new and independent entity, the British Library.

The idea that the Library might be housed in a separate building in fact pre-dated the independent existence of the British Library. The Trustees approved a plan by Sir Leslie Martin and Colin St John Wilson in 1964 to create a piazza to the south of Smirke's museum with a new library in a square building along its eastern side. An enlarged scheme by Wilson alone ran into planning difficulties in 1974 and a year later the new British Library Board accepted the proposal that the Library should instead be built alongside St Pancras Station in Somers Town. In March 1978 the government announced its intention to go ahead with the project.

For the British Museum the benefits resulting from the space that would become available when the Library moved were obvious. For many years, attendance figures had been creeping

*right*
Model of the British Museum Library project to the south of Great Russell Street, proposed by Sir Leslie Martin and Sir Colin St John Wilson in 1964. St George's Church, Bloomsbury, by Nicholas Hawksmoor is seen near the centre

*overleaf*
Interior of the Reading Room, photograph by Frederick York, 1875

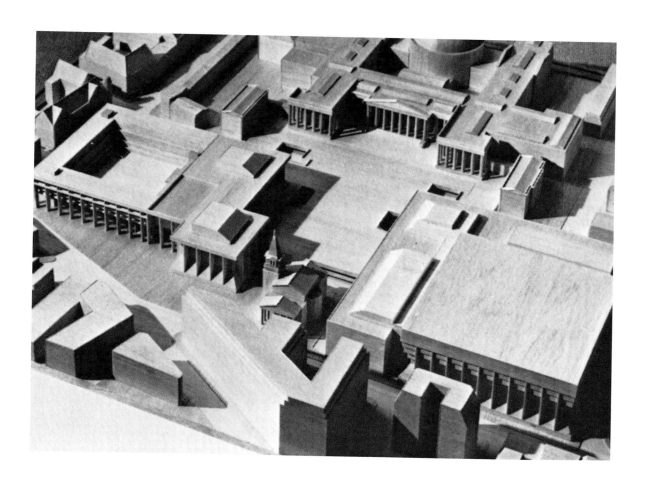

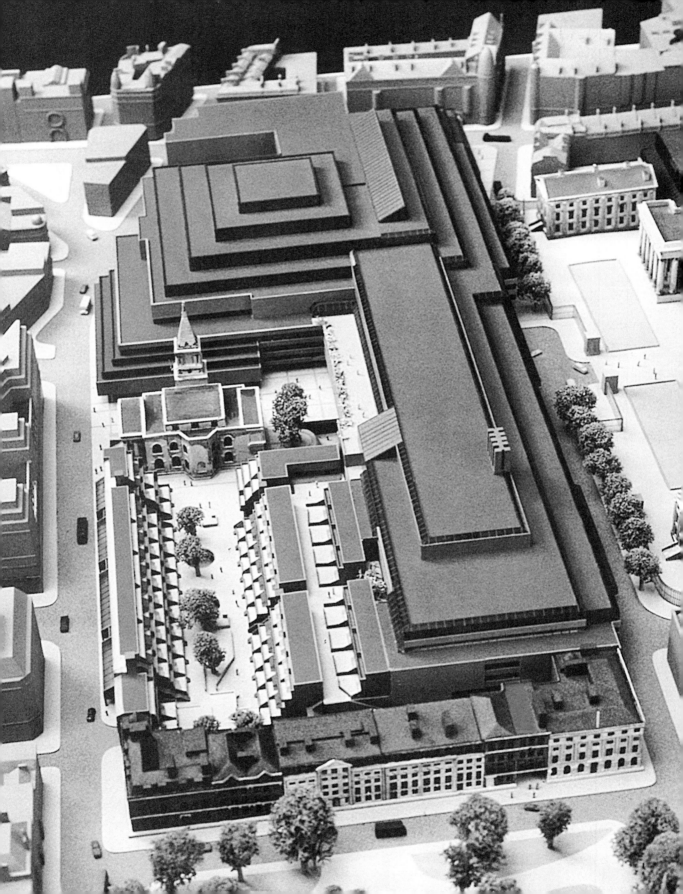

Model of an enlarged scheme for a British Library building to the south of Great Russell Street, drawn up by Sir Colin St John Wilson in 1972

up, and at times the building was becoming too crowded for visitors to concentrate on the exhibits in any comfort. From the 1920s up to the time of the Second World War, there were slightly over one million visits a year. After the Museum re-opened in the late 1940s numbers declined, but reached this level once more in 1962. By 1969 there were more than two million visits annually, and double that by 1977. These figures need to be seen in relation to the level of attendance expected by Smirke, probably 100,000. On a simple floor area calculation, the Library occupied nearly 40 per cent of the space. Clearly, the rewards following the Library's departure would be considerable (though an unexpectedly protracted period of construction would prove to be frustrating for the Museum). A working party under the chairmanship of Sir Arthur Drew, a Trustee, was established in 1979 to determine how the space would best be used by the Museum, but as there was no indication of the date when the new Library would be started, let alone when occupation was likely, and no encouragement had been offered about government funding for the Museum's concomitant costs for adapting and running its additional space, there was an air of unreality about the whole project.

In fact construction of the Library started in April 1982 but the scale of the building was reduced and funding was not consistent on a year-by-year basis. Towards the end of the 1980s the Museum grew increasingly confident that the Library would be moving from Bloomsbury in the reasonably near future and a working party on the future use of the Museum building was set up under the chairmanship of the Trustee and former Permanent Secretary at the Department of the Environment, Sir Peter Harrop. The first meeting was held in June 1989 and five further meetings were held between then and May 1990; the report was assessed by the Board of Trustees in July. The whole of the Museum was considered in the light of the departure of the Library, and from that point of view it was a masterplan. It was the hope of the working party that their recommendations could be substantially achieved by the 250th anniversary of the Museum in 2003, and it was stated that the period during which the Library would vacate its Bloomsbury home would be from 1993 to 1996. The report was wide ranging, but a high priority was to provide much improved public circulation around the Museum. The Reading Room would continue to be used as such, but would house the Ethnographic Library (a particularly large curatorial library) and the Central Library (a general reference library intended to be of value to all Museum staff). The two north bookstacks should be demolished and replaced with a building to house offices and storage facilities for collections. The south-east and south-west quadrant bookstacks would also disappear, to be replaced by an education centre, a lecture theatre, and space for offices for British Museum Publications and the British Museum Friends. In a brochure produced in 1991 to publicize the Harrop plan (as it became known), the Chairman of Trustees, Lord Windlesham wrote, 'The plans are ambitious and will call for a great deal of private generosity and public support. The costs are large, but not unreasonable, and their execution has been planned so as to be spread out over the intervening years [up to 2003].'

In spite of all this preparation, it could not be assumed that the British Museum would automatically take over the vacated Library areas. A business case had to be prepared for the Museum's government sponsor body, the Department of National Heritage (predecessor of the Department for Culture, Media and Sport), and would then be passed on to the Treasury for approval. Government approval was also necessary for a building project of the magnitude that was proposed. Fortunately, these processes ran smoothly, the Museum having strong arguments based on visitor demand, lack of visitor facilities and the need for better public circulation routes. It has to be said that it was difficult to envisage other compatible uses for the lapsed Library spaces, interwoven as they were with the Museum galleries and offices.

The Director of the Museum who had so far overseen the development of the plans, Sir David Wilson, retired in January 1992, to be replaced by Dr Robert Anderson who, when Director of the National Museums of Scotland, had been involved in drawing up a scheme for the Museum of Scotland in Edinburgh, raising funds from the Scottish Office and selecting architects. Shortly after taking up office, Dr Anderson proposed that the Harrop committee be reconvened to consider aspects that he felt needed revisiting, especially the creation of new structures in the courtyard and the use of the Round Reading Room. Concerning

Reconstruction by Foster & Partners of the Reichstag, Berlin (1999), showing the exterior (below) and interior (right) of the glass dome

Four previous designs by Foster & Partners: the Sainsbury Centre for the Visual Arts, University of East Anglia, 1977, above left; the American Air Force Museum at Duxford, Cambridgeshire, 1997, below left; Hong Kong International Air Port at Chek Lap Kok, 1998, above right; and Canary Wharf station, 1998, part of the new London Underground Jubilee Line extension, right

the latter, he argued in a paper to the Trustees that the space should be accessible to all members of the public and that a reference library for general use should be provided. These points were agreed. The question of ethnography had been considered earlier: because of severe problems of overcrowding, the Department of Ethnography had moved from Bloomsbury in 1970 to take up residence in Burlington Gardens, behind the Royal Academy, in an elaborate building originally constructed in 1866 as the Senate House of the University of London. Here it was named the Museum of Mankind. It was always the intention that Ethnography would return when space became available, and the departure of the British Library provided that opportunity. This position was confirmed and plans to bring the Department and its displays back to Bloomsbury were drawn up.

Groups of Museum staff helped to produce the requirements that would be needed in drawing up a brief for an architectural competition. The terms of the competition were considered by the Trustees' Buildings and Design Committee, whose view was that an international competition should be held to identify an architect (rather than a finished design); a 'broad, imaginative view of how the space might be used' was to be sought. The competition was launched in September 1993 and applicants were issued with a brochure that set out the overall guidelines. A selection panel had been appointed by the Board of Trustees, which consisted of Sir Peter Harrop, Mr (later Sir) Michael Hopkins and Sir Claus Moser (all Trustees), Sir William Whitfield (a former Trustee) and Sir Colin Stansfield-Smith (former County Architect to Hampshire County Council). There was a good response, with 132 British and overseas firms declaring interest. In December 1993 a shortlist of twenty-two firms had been selected and by March three had emerged as finalists. These were Arup Associates, Sir Norman Foster & Partners , and Rick Mather Associates. In July 1994 Sir Norman Foster & Partners  were declared the winners and a model of their proposal was shown at the Annual Patrons Dinner on 25 July.

Sir Norman Foster & Partners (now known simply as Foster & Partners), established in 1967, is an internationally renowned architectural firm. At the time of appointment by the Museum it had already received 120 awards and citations for excellence and

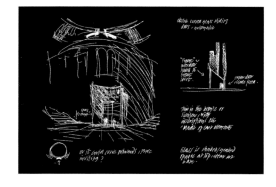

had won 21 international competitions. Its founder, now Lord
Foster of Thames Bank OM, had received the Royal Gold Medal
for Architecture in 1983, the Mies van der Rohe Award for
European Architecture in 1991 and the American Institute of
Architects Gold Medal in 1994. In 1999 he would win the Pritzker
Architecture Prize. Among his major buildings prior to 1994 had
been the Willis Faber & Dumas Head Office in Ipswich, the
Sainsbury Centre at the University of East Anglia, the Hong Kong
and Shanghai Bank in Hong Kong, the Millennium Tower in
Tokyo, the Royal Academy Sackler Galleries, the Stansted Airport
Terminal and the Torre de Collserola, a communications tower in
Barcelona. A project that ran simultaneously with the Great Court
was the reconstruction of the Reichstag in Berlin.

The Foster & Partners scheme for the British Museum was an
admirably simple concept, a vision built on the marriage of
functionality and form. A new floor would be installed at ground
level in the courtyard (which at this time became known as the
'Great Court'), providing the much needed circulation routes.
A roof of Teflon 'pillows' supported in a steel grid would stretch
over the space between the perimeter of the drum of the Reading
Room and the top of the Smirke elevations, creating an internal
covered square. Around the Reading Room would be built an
elliptical structure, the middle floor of which would provide the
two lecture theatres and the seminar rooms sought for an
Education Centre. Access would be provided by a ramp around
the ellipse; on the ground floor of this structure would be a shop
and on the top floor, the restaurant. From the upper part of the
ellipse, three bridges would allow access to the upper galleries of
the Smirke building: to the west into Italy before the Roman
Empire, to the north, Mesopotamia, and to the east, Celtic
Europe. Underground at the front would be a large temporary
exhibition hall; at the back would be an ethnography gallery and
a staff restaurant. At a second basement level would be
collections storage and the kitchens. The Smirke facades, which
over the years had been somewhat damaged by structures put up
in the Great Court (the most recent being the Egyptian 'chapels',
galleries added in 1981), would be restored, except for the long,
metal-framed windows of the north range, which were inserted
during the 1930s mezzanining process. The south portico,

destroyed when the front hall was extended into the Great Court in 1875, would be rebuilt; this would necessitate the removal of the extension together with the accommodation used by the Department of Prehistoric and Romano-British Antiquities (now renamed Prehistory and Early Europe) above it. An important aspect of Foster & Partners' concept was that there should be a through route from the front to the back of the Museum. This would involve the forecourt and the front hall to the south, and beyond the Great Court to the north, the North Library. The Museum forecourt, designed by Sydney Smirke and scarcely changed since its construction in 1850, would be remodelled.

Moving northwards beyond the Great Court was the North Library. Originally designed by Sir Robert Smirke, it was changed significantly at the time of the First World War by the architect Sir John Burnet as a consequence of his adjoining King Edward VII Galleries; worse was to come in the mid-1930s at the hands of the Office of Works. A North Library scheme would later be prepared by Foster & Partners to allow the through route from Great Russell Street to Montague Place (though this was not strictly part of the Great Court project). This would be delivered in two phases, the first to be completed by the time of the opening of the Great Court. Its final manifestation, funded by the Wellcome Trust, would not be fully realized until 2003, when it would become the central display area for Ethnography. A great deal of discussion ensued in the Trustees' Buildings and Design Committee following the presentation of these original ideas. The London Advisory Board of English Heritage and the Royal Fine Arts Commission were consulted so that their views could be taken into account. Fortunately there was ample time for this as the date of completion of the British Library was being pushed further into the future, thereby also providing a realistic programme for the fundraising process. There was a concern that the ellipse occupied too much of the Great Court floor area, and that it stretched rather too close to the entrance through the south portico. As a result, a half-ellipse building was proposed for the north side only, with two monumental staircases leading to it from the south. This meant that the structure was now not large enough to house the Education Centre; as a result this facility was moved underground to replace the large temporary exhibition

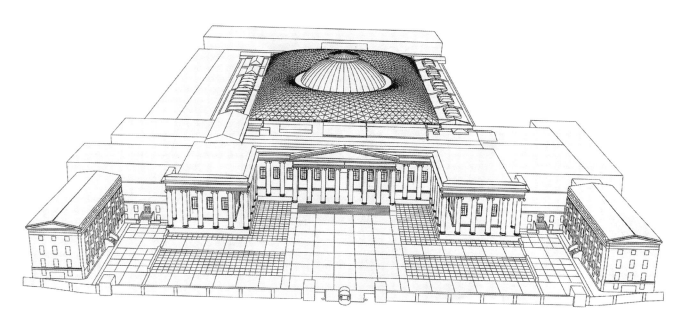

Drawing from the front of the Museum showing the Great Court roof and the unrealized forecourt scheme with stone paving throughout and a broadened path to the steps of the colonnade

hall, and a smaller hall was provided in the ellipse. A later proposal to reduce the bulk of the half ellipse was not adopted because of the consequent reduction in accommodation. Another later suggestion was to replace the traditional staircase with a stepped ramp but this proved impractical. A larger hall could be developed at a later date by extending the existing New Wing Gallery, used since 1978 for special exhibitions. It was decided that though more expensive, a glass roof would be much more desirable than the plastic one first proposed. The east and west bridges were dropped from the scheme as they intruded badly into the north–south views of the facades, though the north bridge was retained. Finally, providing the second basement was going to be a difficult engineering project and very expensive. In 1995 the Museum purchased the nearby Royal Mail Sorting Office in New Oxford Street, which would solve the problem of storage. (This building would later be refashioned as the British Museum Study Centre.) The second basement idea could therefore be abandoned, at the cost of losing the staff restaurant; the kitchens for the public facilities would move up to the first basement level.

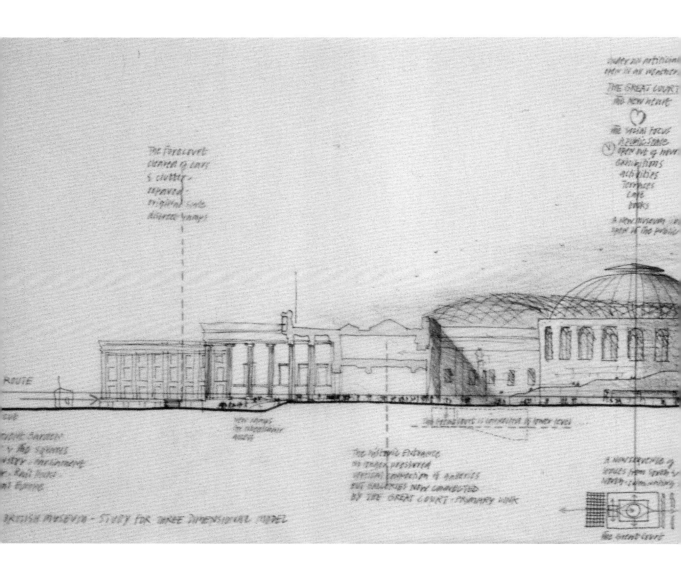

The Forecourt
cleared of cars
& clutter -
repaved -
original scale
restored - ramps

outer & art[illicit]...
open in all weathers.

THE GREAT COURT
the new heart
♡
The social focus
a public space
open but of new
exhibitions
activities
Terraces
Cafe
books

A new museum in
heart of the public

ROUTE

New ramps
to supplement
access

The historic entrance
to index preserved
vertical connection of galleries
the galleries now connected
by the Great Court - primary link

The forecourt is excavated to lower level

A masterpiece of
issues from South &
North - connecting

BRITISH MUSEUM - STUDY FOR THREE DIMENSIONAL MODEL

The latent issue

Cross-section sketch of the Great
Court prepared by Lord Foster,
1999

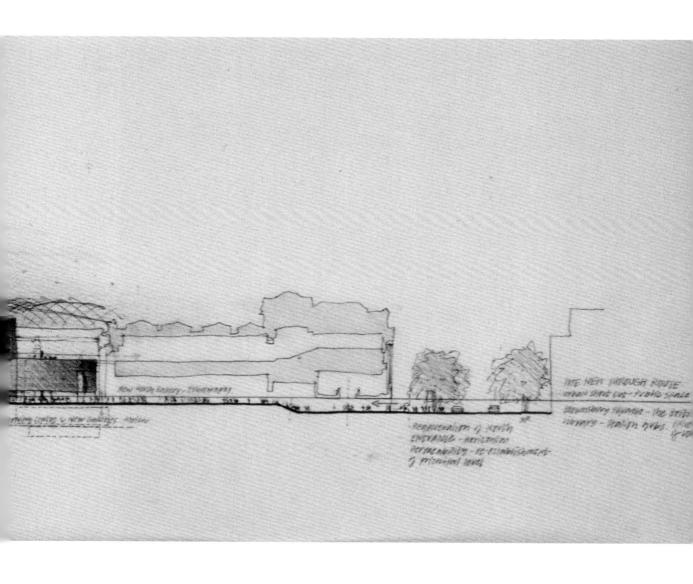

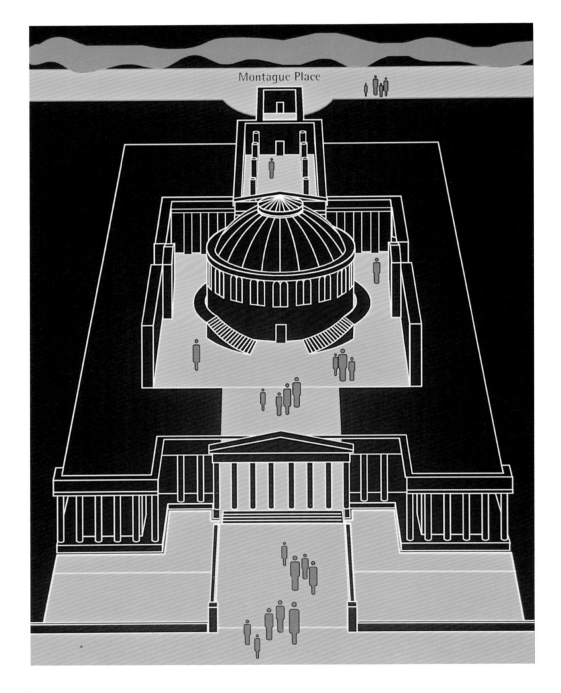

Montague Place

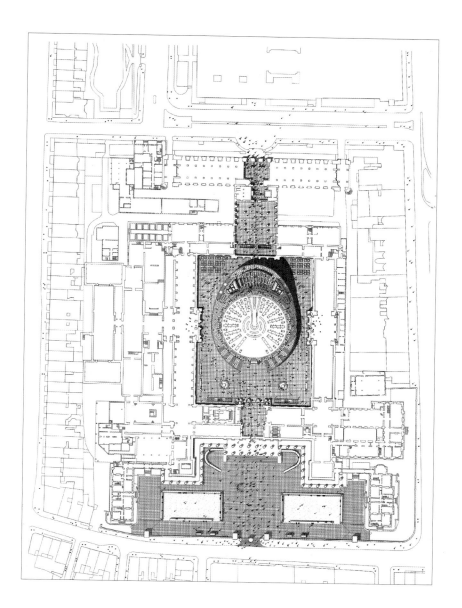

*left*
Impression of the British Museum
from the south showing a
sequence of public spaces
stretching from the forecourt,
through the front hall, Great Court
and North Library, to the Montague
Place entrance

*right*
Plan of the British Museum
showing the final profile of the
Great Court and the forecourt with
the unrealized access ramps for the

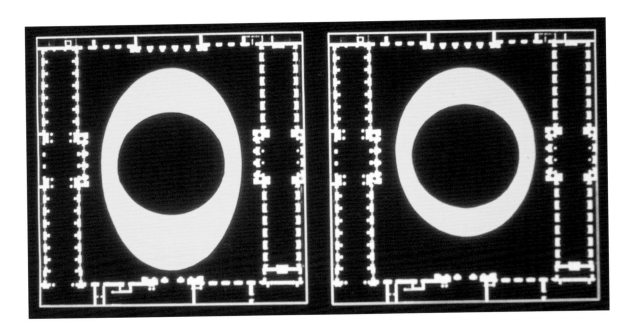

This design work was largely carried out by two architects from Foster & Partners : Spencer de Grey, a partner of the company (who had been the architect in charge of the Sackler Galleries at the Royal Academy and Stansted Airport), and Giles Robinson, a project director. The project sponsor, the Museum executive who acted for the Museum as the project client, was Christopher Jones, Head of Administration. In 1996 the Trustees transferred responsibility for the Great Court from the Buildings and Design Committee to the Great Court Client Committee, chaired by the Chairman of Trustees, Graham Greene. At its first meeting in September it appointed as client project manager Reg Cobham, who had previously been employed as project manager for the erection of oil refineries for BP. His responsibility was to ensure that the construction management firm would build the Great Court to the agreed programme and budget.

Funding was the responsibility of the Museum. The rough cost had originally been estimated at around £60 million, but as the design developed and the work became more detailed, a budget close to £100 million was set, which included all aspects of the project. This was a vast sum to raise, more than ten times the

*above*
The developing profile of Foster's proposals for an elliptical structure around the Reading Room; ultimately, a semi-elliptical construction was adopted

*right*
Discussions at Foster's Riverside offices with the architects (in shirtsleeves) Giles Robinson (right) and Spencer de Grey, client sponsor Chris Jones (behind model), and project manager Reg Cobham (leaning over model)

amount that had been needed for the Japanese galleries which were completed in 1990. Encouragement came in 1994 with the establishment of the National Lottery and the decision by the government that a proportion of the proceeds should be allocated for 'good causes', which included, among much else, capital works for museums and art galleries. The Museum worked hard to put in an early bid to the Millennium Commission and an application was prepared by mid-1995. There was a delay in announcing the outcome owing to continuing uncertainty concerning the move of the British Library, but the government's autumn budget clarifying that funds had been made available for the completion of the St Pancras building helped to elicit a positive response at the beginning of March 1996. 'Lottery's £30m boost for British Museum expansion' was how the *Daily Telegraph* announced the news. The bid had been drawn up so that the scheme was seen not so much as an expansion but as the provision of a covered public square for London (on occasion, the press has referred to the Great Court as a 'piazza'). Because of this emphasis, the commissioners insisted that there should be no admission fee to the Great Court, and that its opening hours had to be significantly longer than those of the surrounding Museum.

The grant of £30 million was certainly significant, and a great boost to the Museum's efforts, but it represented only slightly more than 30 per cent of the total cost. The Museum therefore decided to make a further bid to the Heritage Lottery Fund, the other potential source of Lottery income. This was a complicated matter, as the components of the Great Court that might be funded by the Heritage Lottery Fund had to be quite distinct from those funded by the Millennium Commission. The emphasis in the second bid was therefore directed towards the conservation and restoration of Smirke's quadrangle. It was agreed that the north facade's long metal-framed windows of the 1930s would be restored to Smirke's original design. The ideal solution would have been to restore completely the north range but it was accepted that to re-create Smirke's original room layout was too vast a project to take on. The Heritage Lottery Fund was anxious to persuade the Museum to undertake further restoration work. Though these areas lay outside the Great Court itself, they were nevertheless on the north–south route that was being created through the building. Attention turned to the front hall and staircase, which in 1847 had originally been painted with complex polychromatic patterning, in accordance with mid-Victorian ideas of ancient Greek decorative schemes. Restoration of this decoration had been resisted in the 1980s (and it has to be said that the architectural design was of 1823, not of 1847) but there had been harsh criticism of the Museum at the time, particularly from the Victorian Society and the Georgian Group. Now it was agreed to reinstate the Collman and Davis coloured scheme, and also to replace the railings outside the King Edward VII Galleries that had been removed at the time of the Second World War. The agreement concerning the £15.75 million grant had essentially been finalized by the end of 1997.

The sums that had been agreed meant that the Museum was left with the task of raising more than £52 million if the Great Court was to become a reality. The Museum decided at an early stage that if it was going to succeed in its huge fundraising task, it had to set about the process with considerable specialist involvement. There was already a British Museum trust that had been involved in some work of this kind but it was decided to relaunch it as the British Museum Development Trust. Its first task was to identify a chairman with the necessary experience and drive to make this operation a success. The Chairman of Trustees, Lord Windlesham, and the Director decided to approach Sir Claus Moser, a Trustee who was then Warden of Wadham College, Oxford. Sir Claus had been highly effective in raising money for charitable organizations and educational institutions, including the Royal Opera House (of which he had been chairman from 1974 to 1987) and his own Oxford college. Thus on 12 February 1993 the Chairman and Director bearded the Warden in his den. Sir Claus made a rather poor show of saying how over-committed he was but Mary Moser, arriving with coffee at the *moment juste*, told her husband that of course he would want to take on the role following his retirement that summer. Of the various key moments in the history of the Great Court, this must count as one of the most crucial. Over the next few years Sir Claus Moser and Graham Greene, along with the Director of the Development Trust and the Museum Director, were to spend much time and

Garry Weston, whose Garfield Weston Foundation offered the principal private benefaction of £20 million towards the Great Court

thought preparing the campaign. Many lunches and dinners were taken with potential donors to convince them of the cultural merit and public benefit that would result from the project, while large-scale gala evenings were held to identify future supporters. It was by no means unenjoyable work, and frequently it was exhilarating. Surprisingly few were to turn down our advances. Sir Claus sometimes joked that the list of those who had rejected us was a highly distinguished one, but he had to admit that it was also very short. The Development Trust took over one of the Museum properties, 91 Great Russell Street, and the following year it appointed as its director Dr Gerard Vaughan, at the time Deputy Director of the Campaign for Oxford (University), who had trained as an art historian. HRH The Princess Margaret agreed to serve as Honorary President of the Development Trust, a council of influential public figures was nominated, and a formidable fundraising operation was set in motion. It was a highly successful campaign: pledges for the sum needed, £97.901 million, were identified more than one year before building was completed, and a further £10 million was then raised to allow necessary associated works to be put in hand.

Two other organisations were to provide strong support, both financial and moral. The American Friends of the British Museum was revitalized in 1994 with the appointment of Lawrence A. Fleischman as chairman and the establishment of a staffed New York office on Lexington Avenue. Mrs Leonore H. Annenberg was named as honorary president. Sadly, Larry Fleischman died suddenly during a visit to London early in 1997, but, with Herbert Lucas Jr stepping in for two years, followed by the election of Judith Thomson (Lady Thomson) as chairman, vigorous continuity was assured. The office was moved to a wonderfully located building just off Fifth Avenue which had the use of a small lecture theatre where many a visiting British Museum curator would coax and cajole his audience. The longer-established British Museum Society (in 1999 renamed the British Museum Friends) under its Chairman Nicholas Barber undertook a most successful fundraising exercise for the Great Court among its 12,000 members. The Duchess of Gloucester, as the Friends' patron, gave her time freely for the cause.

Funds in themselves were not enough: a clear building site was

Lord Foster (left) with Sir Claus
Moser, Chairman of the British
Museum Development Trust,
May 1998

HRH The Princess Margaret
with Graham Greene (left) and
Dr Robert Anderson on the roof
of the south-west bookstack,
January 1998

needed and even by the mid-1990s there was still no certainty
about the date of departure of the Library. The booklet *The British
Library and the St Pancras Building*, written in 1994 by the
Chairman of the Library, Sir Anthony Kenny, conveys a sense of
the frustration being felt at that time by our colleagues. Setbacks
had been caused by the quality of some of the components of the
building, and criticisms, many unreasonable, had come from
various interest groups. From the Museum's point of view the
deadline for opening the Great Court had been specified by the
Millennium Commission: December 2000. The building
programme was estimated as being a minimum of two years and
four months, which meant that allowing for time for
commissioning and contingencies, work would have to start on
site by the beginning of March 1998. Understandably, the British
Library did not want to commit itself to a departure date that it
later, possibly through no fault of its own, could not meet. A joint
Museum–Library Committee examined the issues on numerous
occasions until, in its frustration, the Museum sent the Library on
22 May 1997 a timetable that accorded with its own reading of
the situation. This turned out to be a reasonable estimate, and
the dates stuck. In July 1997 the Library started its gargantuan
task of emptying the Museum, where books had been collecting

since 1754. By the end of February the following year the Round Reading Room and its bookstacks had been emptied. Building work started on site shortly afterwards. Builders and book removers worked alongside one another remarkably amicably for several months more until just before Christmas 1998, when the last crate of books left the Bloomsbury site.

Another heroic task needs mentioning: the Great Court and its surrounding spaces were not simply buildings, they contained a plenitude of stores and services, all of which had to be moved and diverted before any of the main construction work could begin. These were known as the Enabling Works. In December 1996 seventy-three separate projects had been identified, and this number was to double. The nature of these projects varied considerably, from the relatively simple removal of the British Museum Rifle Club's range in a sub-basement to the provision of a new energy centre to replace a boilerhouse situated in the Great Court. Much of this work was labour intensive and needed planning to the highest degree, for example the complete emptying of the Prehistoric and Romano-British stores containing the department's reserve collection and its removal, together with its library, to temporary accommodation. The total budget for this essential but unglamorous work was £8.5 million and the work, by a specially formed inter-departmental group, took eighteen months to complete. Nonetheless, it was an essential part of the preparations and affected the work of the whole Museum. But in spite of this, the British Museum was determined to remain open to the public as normal, and this it managed to do despite the vast building project being undertaken at its very heart.

# Construction

Scaffolding erected for the
construction of the Great
Court roof

Building work started in the Great Court on 2 March 1998. Surveys had already been made of the forecourt by museum archaeologists keen to investigate the foundations of Montagu House, which had originally been built in 1675 and from 1754 had been the British Museum's first home. The last complete plan of the basements had been made by the architect George Saunders in 1810, and this helped to define the location of the excavation trenches. Digging revealed that the highest surviving remnant of the house was at a depth three metres below the existing tarmac level, with the lowest being at four metres. No floor surfaces were discovered, and the relative paucity of evidence seemed to support the theory that, when Montagu House was finally demolished in the 1840s, the Trustees sold off everything they could, including brickwork, to assist the financially straitened Museum. A poster in the archives reveals that an auction sale by Messrs Everfield and Horne took place on 21 May 1842 at which 'The Excellent Materials of the North Front of the Old British Museum' were to be disposed of. Few artefacts were recovered, mainly some seventeenth-century pottery sherds and some rather later clay tobacco pipes and a wine glass. Further excavations took place when the opportunity arose. The expected Civil War fortifications in the Great Court itself were not found, to no little relief. Significant quantities of plasterwork were discovered, in the form of both discarded Smirke ceiling decoration and broken casts of antiquities. Later excavations in the forecourt in mid-2000 revealed interesting brickwork foundations, possibly to a design of Robert Hooke, which would have supported the south colonnade of Montagu House. An early water closet was christened 'Hawkins' privy', because it was found in the basement of the residence that had been occupied from 1826 by the Keeper of Antiquities, Edward Hawkins.

Before the builders arrived, the east side of the forecourt was transformed into a construction yard, with areas for depositing and handling materials, offices for the Construction Managers, Mace Limited (who, together with their project manager, Carl Wright, had been appointed to the Great Court professional team in October 1996), and facilities for the workmen who would be operating on site. The great front gates by John Walker of York were removed (possibly for the first time since they had been

*above*
Tony Spence, archaeologist in the Department of Prehistory and Early Europe, examines a fragment of decorative plasterwork excavated from Montagu House

*right*
Demolishing bookstacks, mid-1998

*below*
Nineteenth-century wine or sorbet glass, found intact in the south basement of the former Montagu House, inscribed 'C. Robinson'

opened to the public on 31 May 1852), and a small, temporary set of gates was opened up in the railings to the west, the diminished sense of arrival being somewhat compensated for by the provision of two smart sentry boxes to protect security staff from the elements. On 16 February 1998 the erection of the first tower crane started, to the east of the portico steps. This vast crane, 46 metres (151 feet) high, with a jib 75 metres (246 feet) long (the longest in Europe) and a lifting capacity of 12 tonnes, confirmed both that the project was underway, and that it was a project of great complexity. There being no sizeable entrance to the Great Court from the outside world, practically everything going in or coming out would have to be lifted over the building, a building that on average receives 15,000 visitors every day.

The first significant tasks were demolition and excavation; more than 20,000 cubic metres of material had to be removed. The metre-thick walls of the front hall extension and the solid construction of the bookstacks rebuilt in the 1930s presented considerable difficulties. There were also the logistical problems of removing large quantities of debris out into a busy but small

*above*
Attached columns on the west elevation of the Great Court showing damage caused by earlier construction works

*left*
Constructing ground-floor retail space to the north of the Great Court

*right*
Constructing the Hugh and Catherine Stevenson Lecture Theatre beneath the Great Court

*overleaf*
Cranes over Bloomsbury, early 2000; the 1964 Post Office Tower is to the right

*above*
One of the 1,800 steel nodes,
each of a unique design

*left*
Looking northwards over the
glass-panelled roof towards the
London University Senate House
built by Charles Holden in
1932–7

central London street. Neighbours were invited to a number of meetings to inform them of the scheme and allow them to comment on how their lives were being affected. One part of the operation that needed particular attention was the south-east bookstack, the only one that remained substantially as it had been built, as a cast-iron structure. This was carefully unbolted and the parts marked; though the British Museum had no further use for it, it was hoped that someone might one day wish to resurrect a subsidiary part of the famous Reading Room. Approaches to a number of British and American institutions were unsuccessful, however, and the 'iron library' went into store.

By November 1998 the demolition phase had been completed. Pending excavation to a depth of nearly 10 metres (33 feet), the Reading Room foundations needed careful protection to prevent the now isolated building moving, or worse. Grout, a mixture of water and cement under pressure, was forced into underground gravel layers to prevent this from happening. The Great Court Client Committee received regular reports about the degree of movement of the building and to everyone's relief these were well within the levels of tolerance that had been set. Inside the Museum careful watch was kept of the displayed and stored collections of objects. At an earlier phase of the project, the fourth-century-AD Roman mosaic floor from Hinton St Mary in Dorset had to be taken up from its position in the Central Saloon. This is a particularly precious relic because at its heart it incorporates what might be the earliest surviving image of Christ (the opportunity to display this central roundel as such was later taken to mark the arrival of the end of the second millennium). A number of curatorial departments were forced to remove objects from their galleries, especially sculptures mounted on the walls that formed the perimeter of the Great Court and were particularly prone to vibration arising from the operation of machinery. Dust was another continuing problem but, by and large, staff accepted the difficulties in good spirit.

One operation that needed to start immediately because there was so much of it to be done was the restoration and cleaning of the inner facades. Restoration required a good deal of preliminary research in the Museum's archives amongst Smirke's original drawings to ensure accuracy of detail. The bases of the attached

*above*
The regilded
and repainted dome of
the Reading Room

*left*
Restoring the dome of the
Reading Room

columns of the east and west porticos had been severely damaged in the 1950s and early 1980s respectively. To replace these massive sections, some weighing 4 tonnes, thought had to be given to the huge forces bearing down on them. It was therefore decided to remove the damaged pieces from the peripheries, but to leave the cores, easing in newly carved horseshoe-shaped pieces around the remaining central supports. The bulk of the stonework, however, was in remarkably good condition with sharply defined carved details, considering that it had been exposed for 150 years. However, some rust-coloured stains had appeared, caused by cast-iron cramps holding sections of the masonry together, and rainwater running over lightning conductor strips had resulted in further discolouration. These were removed by jet-spraying the stone with a mixture of water and calcite (a form of crystalline calcium carbonate).

Restoration of the Reading Room was also begun at an early stage, the first task being to box in the original 1857 furniture to protect it until it could be refurbished towards the end of the project. An air-flow system was installed to maintain a carefully controlled environment. The interior of the Reading Room dome was in a poor state of repair, with a clearly visible pattern of cracks needing attention. There had been three efforts at redecoration over the years, the most recent being in 1963, but there was uncertainty as to the original 1857 scheme. The only clue appeared to be a design proposal in the archives which suggested a pattern of gilded guilloche ribs flanked with egg and dart, but examination of the surface under raking light confirmed the suspicion that this scheme had not been followed in every detail. Referring to historical photographs and cross-sections of paint layers, the architectural historians Ian Bristow and Richard Ireland pieced together a stratigraphic chart, which was then tested by scraping away overlaying decoration. Using solvents and scalpels, traces of the original scheme were revealed. It was clearly of a more ornate form than had been anticipated, with gilded palmette, trefoil and guilloche embellishments.

The Reading Room then had to be scaffolded, which was no trivial problem considering the loading constraints on the 'spider', a shallow brick underground vault that forms part of the original innovative ventilation system. A main access platform was built to

Gilding one of the medallion-shaped panels in the roof of the Reading Room dome

Original decorative scheme of the front hall, proposed to the Trustees by means of this watercolour by L. W. Collman in 1846

span the entire room at a height of 7 metres, or 23 feet (just above the galleried bookshelves), with a central tower rising 29 metres (95 feet) into the lantern. The cracks had been repaired in the past, but they had re-opened. A method of filling them with an elastic material reponsive to thermal expansions and contractions was devised by Richard Ireland working with Dr Bill Cooke of the University of Manchester Institute of Science and Technology. It was based on a historical maritime technique known as 'caulking' and used up to the nineteenth century in wooden ships. A flexible material ('Flexiweave') was developed, resembling a surgical bandage, which was applied across the cracks after they had been filled with cotton wadding. The decorative scheme could then be applied using an unconventional zero-tension oil-based paint, which would sit on top of the fabric, rather than be partially absorbed by it. Paint was mixed following analysis of the surviving traces and of a small sample of the original blue found in the archives. Patterns were transferred using stencils, which had to be individually cut to take account of the change in proportions of each guilloche and trefoil, from the narrowest point at the oculus to the widest girth

*above*
Sir John Taylor's front hall extension of 1875, demolished in 1998 to allow restoration of the Great Court

*right*
The front hall staircase redecorated to Collman's scheme, mid-2000

of the dome's base. The unexpectedly large quantity of gold leaf required for this restoration and the hours of skilled labour needed to apply it necessitated a certain adjustment to the Great Court estimates.

Investigations of the original paint surface, similar to those conducted in the Reading Room, were carried out in the front hall by Ian Bristow and Richard Ireland. In fact there is another source of evidence, a detailed watercolour by L.W. Collman, that may have been produced to persuade Trustees of the desirability of the polychromatic patterning when the subject of decoration was discussed in December 1846. Sydney Smirke, by then the Museum's architect, put the idea to them in the following terms: 'If done sparingly and cautiously; in strict conformity with ancient examples, and confined chiefly to the mouldings, I am quite confident of a satisfactory result. Whatever doubt there may be as to the propriety of this kind of embellishment in the exhibition rooms, I apprehend there would be none as to its introduction in the hall and Staircase where there is more architectural effect than in any other part of the interior of the building.'

It seems likely that the original scheme survived (though much retouched) until the 1930s. During the Second World War the staircase ceiling was badly damaged during an air raid; coffered plasterwork was replaced with wood and the original rooflight with an unsatisfactory laylight. There was no attempt to restore the decoration after the war, and the hall and staircase were painted throughout in neutral colours. When Bristow and Ireland examined the paint surfaces with raking light, it became clear that much of the original paintwork survived underneath. Where it was uncovered at various spots by the application of solvents, it was apparent that the decoration adhered very closely indeed to that indicated by the Collman watercolour. Over 200 samples of surviving paint traces were taken for microscopic analysis and the complex design, with all its idiosyncrasies, was reconstructed. Discussions took place as to whether the original scheme should be uncovered and left, or whether it was more desirable to repaint it. Because of the incompleteness of the decoration that remained, it was agreed that the best approach was to paint a reproduction of it on top. Information from all the evidence that had been discovered was transferred to paper, following which

the scheme was replicated on computer. Working from seventy individual pattern drawings, a team of signwriters transferred the designs to the ceiling and walls by the traditional method of 'pouncing', by which the lines of the drawing are pricked through with a spiked wheel and fine charcoal dust is pushed through the holes onto the surface to be painted. The paint was then painstakingly applied within the pattern contours. Not quite every detail of the original scheme survived, and some inspired guesswork, based on the long and detailed experience of the historians working on the project, was necessary. Working conditions were not easy for the painters: the front hall had to be kept open to the public throughout and another ingenious scaffold had to be designed to take account of the needs of all parties.

At the same time as both of these major restoration projects, construction within the Great Court was proceeding. With excavation complete, the two underground sectors started to take shape: the Clore Education Centre to the south and the ethnography galleries to the north, not forgetting the adjacent kitchens that would serve the restaurant on the top of the semi-elliptical building and the cafeterias on the floor of the Great Court. Considering the *tabula rasa* that presented itself to Trustees in the 1820s, it is perhaps surprising that they did not include a lecture theatre in their brief when Smirke was working on his designs. A grand theatre was proposed in the ambitious Burnet scheme of 1904 which wrapped itself around Smirke's building to the west, north and east, but, apart from the King Edward VII Galleries, it was never built. Some provision had previously been made for a lecture theatre in a reconstruction of the Assyrian galleries in the 1890s. Later, in the 1960s, a simple one without raked seating was provided in the basement when the Mausoleum Room had a mezzanine floor inserted. This was a serviceable facility but scarcely one that filled audiences with a feeling of anticipation. The Education Service (later Department) made a relatively late start. Teaching, in the form of lectures, had been provided since the nineteenth century, but it was not until 1972 that the Service was formally established with the appointment of an Education Officer. At the beginning of 1974 offices were provided at 1 Bedford Square. Pressure for

The repainted coffered ceiling of the front hall. Precedents for decorative style and colour scheme were originally sought by Collman from the collections in the Museum

educational provision and facilities started to build up considerably, especially with the advent of the National Curriculum, which made the British Museum a highly desirable target for school parties. In December 1988 the Education Service moved into larger premises at 38 Russell Square. It was not until 1990 that the Museum was able to offer visiting school parties a lunch space, though all that could be provided was one basement room, with schools having to adhere to a strict timetable of short, pre-booked shifts.

The establishment of a dedicated, purpose-built Education Centre was an absolute priority. It needed to be centrally placed, not at the Museum's periphery as had been the case up until then. The Museum asked that two lecture theatres be provided, one large (approximately 350 seats) and one small (150 seats). Though primarily intended for formal presentations, the larger one should be flexible enough to be able to be used for musical and stage performances. The size and capacity of the theatres was limited by the linear distance between the basement ('spider') of the Reading Room and the wall of Smirke's southern facade. Consideration was therefore given to the possibility of building the theatres adjacent to one another, with a common wall that could be moved when large audiences were expected, but this would have produced an uncomfortably shaped space. Associated with the lecture theatres, five seminar rooms were requested, each capable of seating a class or a discussion group during conferences. Later it was decided to dedicate one of these to IT purposes and another to creative activities. A substantial foyer would link all these spaces and there would be places where coffee and tea could be made and refreshments dispensed. The idea was that a course or conference held here could be self-contained, thereby promoting the all-important interaction that invariably takes place after formal presentations have been made. This arrangement did not, however, provide all the kinds of spaces essential for school and family parties: places to deposit coats, prepare for gallery visits, eat sandwiches and muster generally. It had been noticed by the architects that immediately next to the Education Centre, under the Smirke building, was a series of brick-lined vaults used for collections storage and conservation; it would be easy to link these to the Education Centre. The decision

was made, and the result was the creation of the Ford Centre for Young Visitors, halfway down the stairs leading to the Education Centre from the Great Court. At an early stage it had been suggested that there should be a special schools entrance to these facilities, possibly at an underground level. This had been vigorously resisted by the Director on the grounds that children should not be separated off in this way, any more than any other group, and that they should enter the educational areas through the magnificence of the Great Court.

On the other side of the Reading Room, to the north and at an underground level, the three Sainsbury African Galleries have been created for the Ethnography Department. Accessed by stairs that run down from the North Library, they consist of a long rectangular gallery running between two squarer galleries at each end, providing a space with a total floor area of 900 square metres. The walls are plastered and the floor is of oak. A major factor in designing these galleries has been to provide maximum flexibility to allow for changes in the displays. The ethnographic collections contain a higher proportion of objects made of organic materials than any other curatorial department (Prints

and Drawings excepted) and although the light levels can be fully controlled and the atmospheric environment is regulated by an air-conditioning plant, it is desirable to change the displayed material at more frequent intervals than is necessary elsewhere. It is unlikely that objects will remain on display here for more than three years at a time.

The African Galleries contain a particularly strong collection: the material has great chronological breadth and the objects range from the bronze head of a Yoruba King, dating to the twelfth to fifteenth century, to coffins created by the Ga people of southern Ghana and purchased from the craftsmen who made them in April 2000. The displays relate the objects to the societies from which they are drawn, showing how they were created and used, and examine their importance and significance to their owners. They also demonstrate the ways in which African cultures have interacted with each other and with the West. A particular emphasis in the African Galleries is provided by a dedicated area focusing on contemporary works.

Although it is impossible to juxtapose all areas of the collections throughout the Museum in an entirely logical sequence, it is worth noting that the African Galleries are close to the galleries of ancient Egypt and Sudan, and to the John Addis Gallery of Islamic Art, which contains material from the Maghreb (North Africa).

With the underground spaces created, work started on the semi-elliptical building to the north of the Reading Room, a structure that contains accommodation inadequately provided for in the past. At ground-floor level there is a large bookshop and additional shops for guides and souvenirs, one catering specially for children. The bookshop, to the north, is a deep space, which allows for a substantial stock relating to the collections and cultures represented in the Museum. Many of these books are written by curators and generated by the Museum's in-house publisher, the British Museum Press, which produces around sixty new titles each year. The stockholding of the bookshop is 60 per cent greater than was previously possible. The children's shop, in particular, is a considerable improvement on the recent past when it was squeezed into the Assyrian Transept, next to a long-suffering, colossal stone lion from the Temple of Ishtar Sharrat-niphi at Nimrud. The three shops work in harness with two other

adjacent shops, one in the former Grenville Library to the east of the front hall, specializing in replica sculpture, silk and jewellery, and the other just outside the Museum boundary, on the corner of Great Russell Street and Bloomsbury Street.

The middle floor of the semi-ellipse contains the Joseph Hotung Great Court Gallery, a space of 440 square metres positioned between two curves: the circle of the Reading Room and the ellipse of Foster & Partners' building. As with the African Galleries, it is light proof and air conditioned, to allow delicate objects, including loans, to be displayed. The existence of this second temporary exhibition gallery (the other being in the New Wing of 1978) makes it possible for a major exhibition to be always on view to the public. The first Hotung Gallery exhibition to be staged was 'Human Image', which juxtaposed objects representing the human figure and was drawn entirely from the Museum's own collections. This allowed contrasts and comparisons between figures created by different cultures at different times in the past, while presenting a snapshot of the diverse riches amassed by the British Museum over two and a half centuries.

The uppermost space, reached by the staircases that wind their way around the outside of the Reading Room, is occupied by the restaurant. Sitting halfway between the floor of the Great Court and the roof, it allows some remarkable, almost surreal, views of the massive Ionic capitals on the Smirke porticos, together with a

*left*
Reconstructed south portico, September 2000

*below right*
Placing some of the last glass panels in the roof, mid-2000

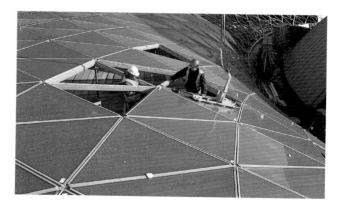

Computer-generated side view of
the Great Court roof prepared by
Buro Happold

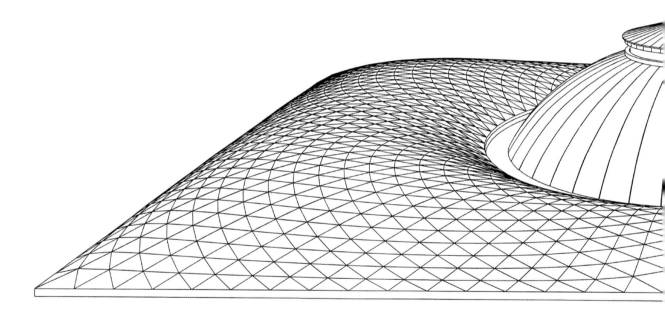

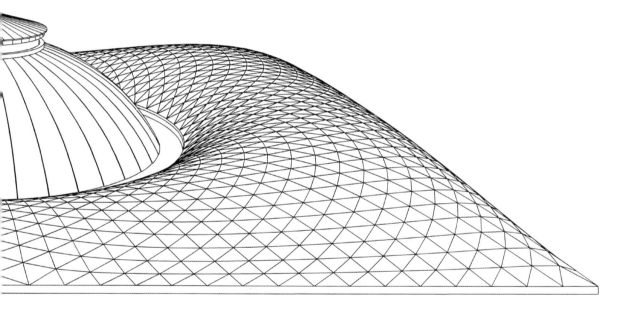

glimpse through the Reading Room windows to the restored inner surfaces of the dome and the readers below. Around the outside of the restaurant runs the route that leads to the bridge, taking the visitor at upper-floor level into Mesopotamia and on via the Egyptian Funerary Galleries and the Coptic Egypt Corridor to the Japanese Galleries, the Prints and Drawings Galleries, the Korea Foundation Gallery and the Joseph Hotung Gallery of Oriental Antiquities in the King Edward VII building. The advantage of this entirely new access route is that it draws parts of the Museum closer together. The whole of the Reading Room and the semi-elliptical building are clad with a Spanish limestone, Galicia Capri, in a simple stack bond. The exterior of the Reading Room was never visible to the public in the past. The cladding at an upper level was an ochre-coloured London stock brick, while at the lower level there was no cladding at all because of the four attached bookstacks. The external windows to the Reading Room had ugly rectilinear metal frames and bore no relationship to the elegant arched fenestration within. Thankfully these have now gone, and readers can gaze at the sky through the glazed roof from their desks.

A further long-term operation was the re-creation of the south portico, demolished in 1875 when the front hall was extended. The design, the manufacture and the installation of its replacement were all major tasks, and although Smirke's original drawings survive, it was not simply a matter of copying what had been there before. One of the problems was access through it from the front hall. In Smirke's day only a domestic-sized doorway was necessary, as few of the mere 100,000 visitors a year would have wanted to enter the garden. In the year 2000 and beyond, on the other hand, it is conjectured that most of the six million or more visitors will wish to pass into the Great Court. For that reason, three substantial openings have been provided between the attached columns. Decorative mouldings and architraves have been copied from other Smirke designs. Moreover, it was thought very desirable to offer views from the Central Saloon into the Great Court at the upper level, and this has been provided by means of a single square opening. A further problem has been providing lift access to the upper floors at the front of the Museum. One way of doing this was to build liftshafts in the

*above*
Computer image of the final design for the Great Court roof

*right*
Looking to the south over the the Great Court roof, with the pediment of Smirke's forecourt portico showing beyond the Reading Room dome. The wheel of the 'London Eye' is visible on the horizon to the right

*overleaf*
Working from temporary decking to construct the roof

depth of the portico itself, but this could only be done by thickening the dimensions of the portico, thereby thrusting it into the Great Court to a greater degree than in Smirke's design. All these matters were discussed at length with English Heritage and the Heritage Lottery Fund, with Professor David Walker, architectural historian and adviser to the latter, being particularly involved. After much debate, largely enjoyable, agreement was eventually reached.

Construction of the portico on site started somewhat later than planned, in March 1999. Preparations for this moment had included identifying blocks of stone large enough to be carved, and making latex moulds of details of Smirke's east portico so that copies could be created. The operation was one of the largest masonry constructions undertaken in recent decades, requiring some 2,000 tonnes of limestone. Concern was expressed that the stone had not been excavated from the quarries at Portland, but was instead a mineral called Anstrude Roche Claire, derived from a French source. Although this was allowed for within the tender specification (the requirement was for 'oolitic limestone, Portland base-bed or similar') it had been understood that Portland stone was being supplied. The Chairman of English Heritage, Sir Jocelyn Stevens, complained about this and about other aspects of the portico's construction. This was followed by a significant amount of comment in the press over several months. Though the colour of the newly cut and carved stone is somewhat different from the surrounding, weathered Portland stone, it has to be remembered that the south portico is both of very recent construction and not made to exactly the original design by Smirke. Whatever view is taken, the additon of the south portico is a vital component in the re-establishment of the integrity of Smirke's concept.

Perhaps two aspects are particularly striking to visitors on entering the Great Court through the south portico: the sense of space and the design of the roof. The volume is surprisingly large; in fact two acres are enclosed by the Smirke galleries, the highest point of the roof being 26.3 metres (86 feet) above floor level. Many visitors who have been coming to the Museum for years have not appreciated that a central, inaccessible space existed at all. The roof, in some ways the key to the Great Court, went

*above*
Suzanna Taverne, Managing Director of the British Museum, with representatives from Foster & Partners, Buro Happold and Waagner-Biró working together to remove the last roof support

*right*
Sinuous curves of roof steelwork seen from the decking; each of the 3,312 panels of glass possesses a unique shape

*below*
Cleaning the exterior of the roof

through multitudinous phases of development. There were many geometrical complexities to be considered, one being the surprising lack of symmetry about the Great Court itself. The Reading Room is not centrally placed, being about 5 metres to the north of the point at which the diagonal axes intersect. The height of the pediments, over which the roof would have to stretch, are different. The intention of the architects and the engineers who took on the technical aspects of the design, Buro Happold (led by Stephen Brown), was to create as light and airy a structure as possible, while taking into account its effect on the whole roofline of the Museum when viewed from surrounding streets. The initial design, presented to the Great Court Client

*above*
The builders were on site for 33 months, and on some days there were as many as 600 at work on the Great Court

*left*
The junction between the old and the new: 1823 neo-Grecian Smirke facade meets year 2000 Foster roof

Committee in October 1996, included steeply inclined glazing around the perimeter of the drum of the Reading Room (so that the roof could gain the height it needed to span the pediments), before the profile flattened out. On the main steel structure there would be separate fixings to hold double-glazed glass panels in place. This early concept was developed further and went through another process of evolution. The design that eventually emerged was of a continuous, highly curved torus, rather like a square doughnut with a hole through its middle. During this process the number of triangular glazed panels increased and decreased, finally settling at 3,312, each one unique. It was shown that the glass could be attached directly to the main steel structure, which helped to create a feeling of lightness. The finished design consisted of a series of interconnecting arcs whose shape varies according to the ratio between their height and the distances between the Reading Room and the Smirke facades. This lengthy design process would scarcely have been possible without the use of a sophisticated form-generating computer programme.

Wind tests conducted at Bristol University verified the mechanical properties of the design. Because of the potential effects of thermal gain, fritted dots of white ceramic were sealed into 56 per cent of the surface of the tinted glass, ensuring that only 25 per cent of the incident radiation enters through the glass, though a larger proportion than this is in the visible range of the spectrum. The roof rests on twenty new columns built around the circumference of the Reading Room and hidden behind the stone cladding, while around the facades it is supported by sliding bearings which themselves rest on a structure supported by squat steel columns running down to a new, reinforced-concrete parapet beam. This allows for thermal expansion and contraction of the roof to occur.

To erect the roof, a tall platform had to be built across the whole courtyard, which took on the appearance of a dense forest of scaffolding poles. Components of the roof structure, made from Grade D high-purity steel and manufactured in Vienna by the firm Waagner-Biró to a precise specification, were then shipped to Derby where they were made up into 152 prefabricated sections ('ladders'). Over a six-month period they were lifted into place over the Museum building. In all, 5,200 steel members had to be welded to 1,800 metal nodes, each one different. The individual glass panels were then fixed into their unique positions in the steel framework. When the structural lattice was complete and the glass installed, the temporary props that supported it were systematically removed. As calculated and in a most satisfactory manner, the whole roof then dropped 150 millimetres (6 inches) and spread 90 millimetres (3.5 inches) laterally, as it settled onto its sliding bearings and became self-supporting. The whole structure weighs a total of nearly 800 tonnes – 478 tonnes of steel and 315 tonnes of glass – and yet the impression it gives is one of lightness, even fragility.

The final major task was the laying of the floor (of a French limestone, Balzac), though the concrete substratum had been in place for some time before this was started. In fact, there had never been a floor structure in the Great Court in the past, except in the Reading Room; this was because the area had originally been occupied by the garden, which was laid out at half a level

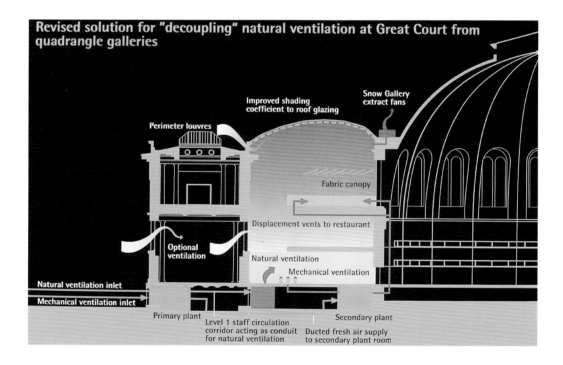

## Revised solution for "decoupling" natural ventilation at Great Court from quadrangle galleries

Improved shading coefficient to roof glazing

Snow Gallery extract fans

Perimeter louvres

Fabric canopy

Displacement vents to restaurant

Optional ventilation

Natural ventilation

Mechanical ventilation

Natural ventilation inlet

Mechanical ventilation inlet

Primary plant

Level 1 staff circulation corridor acting as conduit for natural ventilation

Secondary plant

Ducted fresh air supply to secondary plant room

below the ground floor of the front hall and galleries. Between the concrete and limestone is a labyrinth of pipework through which hot or cold water flows to provide heating on the coldest days and cooling on the hottest. After the last visitor has departed at night, clean, treated air is drawn in from ventilation shafts below, displacing the stale air from the Great Court through vents around the upper perimeter of the drum.

The physical construction of the Great Court has resulted in a profound transformation of a hidden and lost courtyard into what some will identify as the major architectural feature of the Museum. To some extent this has adjusted Smirke's concept, but it has also restored much of it. What is undeniable is that such development was essential if the British Museum was to be able to offer visits of greater comfort and benefit, and to an even wider audience, than in the past. Now the Museum has an accessible nucleus that not only encourages movement through the building but offers facilities that it sorely lacked in the past. The very heart, however, is more contemplative. The Reading Room offers a different kind of experience, complementary to those traditional museum discoveries that can be made in the galleries that encircle the Great Court. It is the introduction of this variation and choice that marks a further stage of development, another new beginning, both symbolic and practical, for the British Museum.

Diagram showing the environmental air-flow control system designed by Buro Happold

# Realization

The Reading Room newly clad in
Galicia Capri limestone

THE GREAT COURT was not intended, nor should it be understood, as simply an additional space made available within an overstretched museum. While it is true that rising numbers of visitors placed excessive strains on the existing resources, especially on the gallery spaces (which had to act as both locations for display and routes of access), the Great Court was developed to offer a new kind of museum-going experience. Just as Smirke's building was in no sense meant to be a Montagu House on a larger scale, so the Great Court offers a departure from the restrictions of Smirke's design, not simply in terms of floor area but in the way a visit to the British Museum is perceived. Until the Great Court existed, the route through the Museum was uncompromisingly linear. One culture and one presentation of the collections followed the other in a relentless progression. To reach a different gallery, it was frequently necessary to retrace one's steps, incommodiously experiencing everything again, but in reverse order. The Great Court has changed this, allowing visitors to wander in and out of the galleries, if they wish, from a space at the heart of the museum. In addition, the Great Court offers the possibility of refreshment, literally and metaphorically. It allows for changes of mood and atmosphere during the course of a visit, thereby enriching the visitor's experience of the British Museum, or it stands alone as a destination it its own right.

Other innovatory developments have led to a variety of new experiences. That does not mean to say, however, that there has been any erosion in the traditional values that are espoused. The Museum's *Review 2000* was able to state, quite truthfully, 'Against the background of major renewal, the British Museum has maintained a full programme of education, gallery refurbishment, exhibitions, scholarship and collections management, and made some outstanding acquisitions.' During the year in question, some 66 books were published by the British Museum Press and 220 articles were contributed to scholarly journals. *Review 2000* lists 37 temporary exhibitions available during the course of the year and the locations of 41 fieldwork or excavation projects in the United Kingdom or abroad with which the Museum was associated. All this was

COMPASS (Collections Multimedia Public Access System) is the most detailed online guide yet produced by any museum for the general public. It is available on fifty computer terminals in the Walter and Leonore Annenburg Information Centre in the Reading Room as well as on the Web.

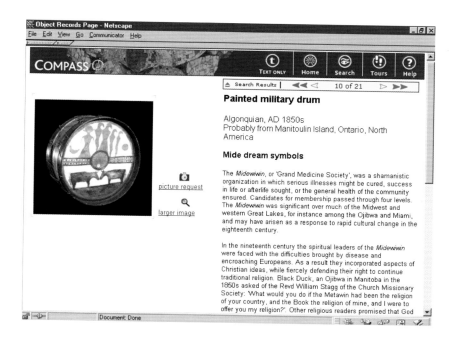

**COMPASS**

TEXT ONLY | Home | Search | Tours | Help

### Painted military drum

Algonquian, AD 1850s
Probably from Manitoulin Island, Ontario, North
America

### Mide dream symbols

The *Midewiwin*, or 'Grand Medicine Society', was a shamanistic
organization in which serious illnesses might be cured, success
in life or afterlife sought, or the general health of the community
ensured. Candidates for membership passed through four levels.
The *Midewiwin* was significant over much of the Midwest and
western Great Lakes, for instance among the Ojibwa and Miami,
and may have arisen as a response to rapid cultural change in the
eighteenth century.

In the nineteenth century the spiritual leaders of the *Midewiwin*
were faced with the difficulties brought by disease and
encroaching Europeans. As a result they incorporated aspects of
Christian ideas, while fiercely defending their right to continue
traditional religion. Black Duck, an Ojibwa in Manitoba in the
1850s asked of the Revd William Stagg of the Church Missionary
Society: 'What would you do if the Metawin had been the religion
of your country, and the Book the religion of mine, and I were to
offer you my religion?'. Other religious readers promised that God

picture request

larger image

Document: Done

---

achieved at a time of intense activity surrounding the building
of the Great Court and preparing for its operation.

Perhaps the most prominent of the developments are those to
be found in the Round Reading Room. Before the completion of
the British Library there were calls for the Reading Room to be
retained by the Library solely for the use of its readers; there were
even suggestions that there should be an underground tunnel
built between St Pancras and Bloomsbury to allow books to be
moved between the two institutions. These proposals were
entirely impractical, but the Museum was anxious that the
Reading Room would be retained for its original purpose.
However, it would not just be for readers with specialist needs,
but for a more general public who wished to combine viewing the
collections with consultation of the books, thereby enhancing the
museum experience by extending their knowledge and
understanding. Although a number of museums provide access to
their libraries, few have developed book collections with the
ordinary museum-goer, young and old, in mind. A new book
stock, projected to contain 25,000 volumes, is being created

especially for this purpose, concentrating on publications that deal with artefacts and, more generally, world cultural history, together with general reference works. The British Museum has been anxious to make this most inspiring of places available to everyone, without the need for registering readers and issuing readers' tickets. Anyone can walk in. The front section of the Reading Room is intended to offer the visitor some of the history of the place. From 1857 to 1998 the Reading Room was used by a large proportion of the best-known British writers, scholars and intellectuals, and quite a number of their foreign counterparts too. A very brief list might include Matthew Arnold, Walter Bagehot, Samuel Beckett, Hilaire Belloc, Fernand Braudel, Robert Browning, Sir Arthur Conan Doyle, Sir Edward Elgar, Sir Jacob Epstein, Michael Faraday, Robert Frost, Mrs Gaskell, Graham Greene, Gustav Holst, T.H. Huxley, John Keble, Rudyard Kipling, Lenin, Karl Marx (who famously wrote *Das Kapital* in the Reading Room), Lewis Mumford, George Orwell, Sir Nikolaus Pevsner, Karl Popper, Dante Gabriel Rossetti, John Ruskin, George Bernard Shaw (who left part of his estate to the British Museum, 'in acknowledgement of the incalculable value to me of my daily resort to the Reading Room at the beginning of my career'), Gertrude Stein, Marie Stopes, Sun Yat-Sen, Alfred, Lord Tennyson, Leon Trotsky, Kenneth Tynan, Ralph Vaughan Williams, H.G. Wells, Virginia Woolf, W.B. Yeats and Israel Zangwill. Books written by these authors and many others who used the Reading Room line the bookshelves in this area, which has been set aside for those visitors who simply wish to view this remarkable space with all its literary associations.

Another new and innovative facility available in the Reading Room is COMPASS (Collections Multimedia Public Access System). The British Museum embraced the IT revolution from its beginnings: the programme to transfer records of objects into computerized form started over twenty years ago, largely for the use of professionals in the museum world. Since 1997, however, a project has been developed that enables the general public to explore the collections to gain a fuller understanding of objects and their contexts. This is the COMPASS database, which harnesses three-dimensional imaging, computer modelling and

Re-opened Reading Room, with Ethnography Library on the upper shelves and Hamlyn Library below

video and is available at fifty terminals in the Reading Room. The selection of the initial 4,000 objects on the database was guided by the thousands of public enquiries made to the Museum every year, and by the needs of schools, especially those generated by the National Curriculum. In fact, school groups can access COMPASS from their own IT room in the Clore Education Centre. Users can choose those artefacts that interest them, find out who made them, why and when, and generally learn about the cultures that produced them. They can then create their own personal tour through the Museum and have maps printed out to guide them through the galleries to see the objects they have chosen. A British Museum smart card allows visitors to purchase print-outs and photocopies; on returning to the system in the future, they will find that their selected artefacts and other system preferences have been saved. Since June 2000 part of the system has been available on the Web (www.thebritishmuseum.ac.uk) for those around the world who are unable to visit the Museum in person. Thus a facility developed for the Great Court has now become one of the Museum's most important outreach activities.

Computer-generated view of Anish Kapoor's stainless steel sculpture, *Turning the World Upside Down*, in front of the original entrance to the Reading Room

The connecting thread throughout the Great Court is supplied by that perhaps overused word 'access'. First of all there is straightforward physical access. The Great Court will be free to all who wish to come, without an admission charge, continuing that noble and beneficial tradition established by the first Board of Trustees in 1753. Access for the disabled has been carefully considered throughout the planning stages, and discussions have been held with representatives of the disabled community by the Museum's Access Officer. Inside all the newly created spaces access is made possible at all levels by the provision of lifts. A particular problem has always been the steps in front of the Museum; the mechanically operated platform located alongside the steps is not now seen as the best solution and this issue continues to be worked on. The hours of admission to the Great Court are generous, closing time being 6.00 pm on Sunday, 9.00 pm on Monday to Wednesday and 11.00 pm on Thursday to Saturday. At the same time, museum hours are being extended, with late-night openings on every Thursday and Friday. The Clore Education Centre allows unprecedented intellectual access through its multiple spaces for direct teaching, film, performance and creative projects. The new facilities mean that there is space for 250,000 children a year in pre-booked parties, and there is in place a sizeable programme of adult and evening events, many organized by the flourishing British Museum Friends. The Curatorial and Education Departments have developed a stimulating programme of conferences, the proceedings of many of which are published, permitting the Museum to influence scholarly debate worldwide.

The British Museum can be a baffling place topographically, although the very existence of the Great Court brings a coherence and logic to the building. To improve matters significantly, a signage strategy was developed in the Great Court and elsewhere in the Museum, with clear, unambiguous directions being shown on 'stelae', tall thin vertical boards. The lettering, in a highly readable typeface (Bliss), conforms to the Museum's new corporate image launched in spring 2000. Other information about the Museum is available from staff stationed at two circular desks situated to the right and left on entry to the courtyard.

A particularly striking feature on entering the Great Court, apart from the sheer volume and remarkable architecture, is the tall, polished-steel elliptical sculpture by the acclaimed sculptor Anish Kapoor. Entitled *Turning the World Upside Down*, it is placed on the main axis of the space, just in front of the original, diminutive doorway of the Reading Room, and produces strange optical effects. The Kapoor is the only contemporary sculpture in the Great Court, but there are a variety of other pieces drawn from the collections. The sculptures are all free-standing and have been chosen to give visitors an impression of the historical and cultural range available through the curatorial departments. To the front are two massive classical sculptures: the Lion of Knidos and a Roman horse and rider. To the north is a stela of Ashurnasirpal, from Nimrud, and a statue from Easter Island. In addition, striking works mark the entrances to the Egyptian sculpture gallery, the North Library and the King's Library, these being respectively two heads of Amenophis III, Mayan stelae and statues of Chinese envoys, and a pair of Ogham stones from Cork.

The existence of the Great Court has stimulated new attitudes and approaches to the operation of the Museum. These have been masterminded by the Managing Director, Suzanna Taverne, appointed in 1999, who with the new Director of Marketing and Public Affairs, Carol Homden, and other members of the management board team has developed an ambitious and comprehensive five-year plan to ensure the effective running, promotion and use of the space and of the Museum's rich and varied exhibition programme for the benefit of all visitors. The Great Court, while making sense in itself in relation to the Museum around it, needs to be regarded alongside future schemes that have been planned but have yet to be implemented. Within the Bloomsbury building itself, the most important of these are the King's Library project and the completion of the suite of ethnography galleries. A short distance away, in New Oxford Street, is the biggest of these schemes, the Study Centre. The intention is that this will be largely completed by the time the Museum celebrates its 250th anniversary in 2003, while the refurbished King's Library will be a centrepiece of the celebrations.

Sculpture in the Great Court (opposite, top) Roman horse and rider, 1st and 2nd centuries AD; (opposite, below) Easter Island statue known as Hoa Hakananai'a, c. AD 1000; (above) marble lion from Knidos, late 4th century BC

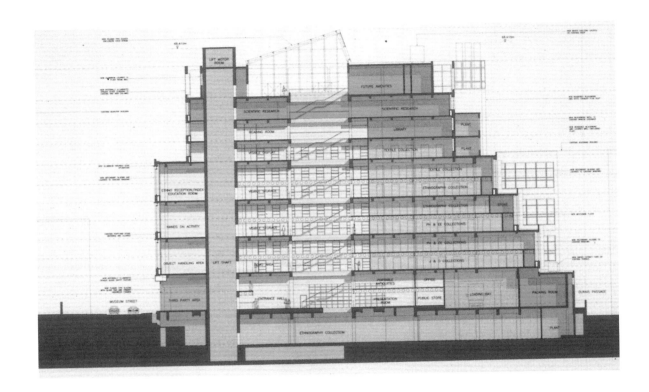

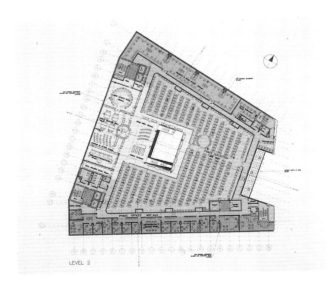

LEVEL 2

Three views of architectural proposals for the interior of the Study Centre, to be developed from 2001 to 2004 in the former Royal Mail Sorting Office in New Oxford Street, originally designed by E.T. Serjent and built 1961-9

NORTH/UT CONSERVATION
STUDIOS / WORKSHOPS

LIBRARY & OFFICE ABOVE COLLECTION
STORES BELOW

MULTI-HEIGHT
STUDY ATRIUM

LIBRARY & OFFICE ABOVE COLLECTION
STORES BELOW

DEPARTMENTAL
OFFICES/MEETING ROOMS

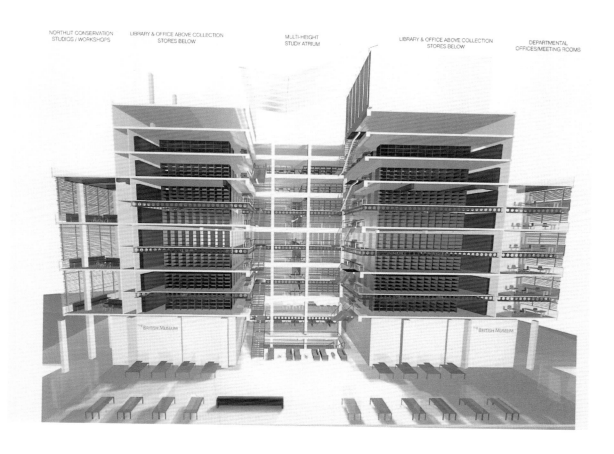

Furthermore, the North Library will become the Wellcome Gallery of Ethnography. In the sense that all artefacts in the Museum can be considered 'ethnographic', and the fact that the space is adjacent to the Great Court and on part of the main route through the building, the Wellcome Gallery will assume considerable significance. Perhaps, though, it is the Study Centre that will make the most difference, for it is here that most of the Museum's collections will be stored (though still remaining easily accessible to the public), and here that four of the curatorial departments and the two scientific departments will be accommodated. The Study Centre will not incorporate galleries or exhibitions proper, though it will be a part of the Museum that will regularly be sought out by the public. Just as the new Reading Room library bridges a gap for those who want to read more about subjects that fascinate them, so the Study Centre will facilitate further levels of understanding about the objects in the collections, providing a behind-the-scenes look at the Museum in action. For example, how is something that has been dug out of the ground by an archaeologist made intelligible and provided with a context as valuable evidence of human activity? How is it best preserved for future generations, so that it can continue to yield clues to the past? How do textiles or ceramics made by different cultures relate to one another? It is clear from the Museum's experience that many members of the public are interested in these sorts of questions and in others like them. The Study Centre will be an invaluable and unique resource for such people, and for new audiences.

In considering the future, and the fundamental purpose of museums, it is appropriate to recall a particularly apposite quotation from a former user of the Reading Room which has been set in the limestone floor of the Great Court and provides a fitting conclusion to this survey:

> and let thy feet,
> millenniums hence
> be set in midst of knowledge
>
> Tennyson

Nelson Mandela and Graham Greene, 16 November 2000. Mr Mandela lectured on 'World Civilization' at the inauguration of the BP Lecture Theatre in the Clore Education Centre

# Donors

Those listed below generously provided the financial support which was required for the project. Their names are inscribed on the Reading Room drum.

**Principal Benefactor**
The Weston Family

**Foundation Grants**
The Millennium Commission
Heritage Lottery Fund

**Benefactors of the Great Court**
American Friends of the British Museum
Walter and Leonore Annenberg
`Asahi Shimbun
BP
The British Museum Company
The Clore Foundation and The Vivien Duffield Foundation
Sir Joseph Hotung
Donald and Jeanne Kahn
Peter Moores
Sir Robert and Lady Sainsbury
David and Susie Sainsbury

**Major Donors of the Great Court**
The Paul Hamlyn Foundation
The Headley Trust
The Kresge Foundation
The Monument Trust
The Henry Moore Foundation
Raymond and Beverly Sackler
Hugh and Catherine Stevenson

**Major Supporters of the Great Court**
The Alaghband Foundation
James and Julie Alexandre
The Deborah Loeb Brice Foundation
The British Museum Friends
The John S. Cohen Foundation
Jean Duffield
The John Ellerman Foundation
The Equitable Charitable Trust
The Esmée Fairbairn Charitable Trust
James Fairfax
The Fidelity Foundations of Fidelity Investments
Flemings
The Horace W. Goldsmith Foundation
The International Friends of the British Museum
Marconi
Gad and Birgit Rausing
The Rayne Foundation
The Coral Samuel Charitable Trust
Schroders
Paul Thackray
The Eugene V. and Clare E. Thaw Charitable Trust
The Trusthouse Charitable Foundation
Harry Weinrebe
The Weinstock Fund
Anthony and Jane Weldon
The Maurice Wohl Charitable Foundation

# Bibliography

## Books

R.G.W. Anderson, 'Renewing a Great Institution', in Yung-Yuan Chen (ed.), *Museum and Architecture: Toward a New Museum* (National Museum of History: Taipei 2000) pp. 11-43.

Michael Brawne, *Neue Museen: Planning und Einrichtung* (Gerd Hatje: Stuttgart 1965)

*British Museum Review 1996/1998* (The British Museum: London [1999])

*British Museum Review 2000* (The British Museum: London 2000)

Marjorie Caygill, *The Story of the British Museum* (British Museum Press: London 1992)

Marjorie Caygill and Christopher Date, *Building the British Museum* (British Museum Press: London 1999)

J Mordaunt Crook, *The British Museum* (Allen Lane: London 1972)

Anthony Kenny, *The British Library and The St Pancras Building* (The British Library: London 1994)

Jonathan King (ed.), *Human Image* (British Museum Press: London 2000)

Edward Miller, *That Noble Cabinet: A History of the British Museum* (Deutsch: London 1973)

Nikolaus Pevsner, *A History of Building Types* (Thames and Hudson: London 1976)

Malcolm Quantrill, *The Norman Foster Studio* (E. & F.N. Spon: London 1999)

Colin St John Wilson, *The Design and Construction of the British Library* (The British Library: London 1998)

David M. Wilson, *The British Museum: Purpose and Politics* (British Museum Publications Ltd: London 1989)

## Pamphlets

*A Celebration of Two and a Half Centuries: A Plan for the British Museum* [1990]

*The British Museum: Guidelines for the Future Use of the Inner Courtyard* [1993]

*The Heart of the British Museum: the Selection of a Consultant Architect* (1994)

*British Museum Great Court Newsletter*, issues 1-5 (under different titles), Winter 1997/98 – Autumn 1999

*The British Museum 2003: Celebrating 250 Years* (1998)

*The British Museum Study Centre* (1999)

## Manuscripts

Papers and Plans in the British Museum generated by the Great Court project, 1990-2000

## Photographic Credits

The author and publishers are very grateful to the following for providing photographs for this book.
The British Museum Photographic Service (in particular, photographers Dudley Hubbard and Simon Tutty); Foster and Partners (in particular, photographers Richard Davies, Dennis Gilbert and Nigel Young); and Buro Happold.
Illustrations are also reproduced by courtesy of the following:
© Newspaper Publishing plc (p. 13); © Mann (p. 31); © Professor Colin St John Wilson (p. 34); © Times Newspapers ltd (p. 58, top); © Telegraph Group Limited (p. 69).

# Index